ROW

BY

ROW

TERRY MARTIN

Martingale
& C O M P A N Y
BOTHELL, WASHINGTON

Credits

President . . . . Nancy J. Martin
CEO . . . . Daniel J. Martin
Publisher . . . . Jane Hamada
Editorial Director . . . . Mary V. Green
Editorial Project Manager . . . . Tina Cook
Technical Editor . . . . Darra Williamson
Copy Editor . . . . Liz McGehee
Design and Production Manager . . . . Stan Green
Illustrator . . . . Laurel Strand
Photographer . . . . Brent Kane
Cover Design . . . . Magrit Baurecht
Interior Design . . . . Jennifer LaRock Shontz

Martingale & Company
PO Box 118
Bothell, WA 98041-0118 USA
www.patchwork.com

That Patchwork Place is an imprint of
Martingale & Company.

Printed in China
05 04 03 02 01 00   6 5 4 3 2 1

Library of Congress Cataloging-in-Publication Data

Martin, Terry
   Row by row / Terry Martin.
      p. cm.
   Includes bibliographical references and index.
   ISBN 1-56477-305-1
      1. Patchwork–Patterns. 2. Patchwork quilts. I. Title.

TT835.M27363 2000
746.46'041—dc21   00-055009

> ## Mission Statement
>
> We are dedicated to providing quality products and service by working together to inspire creativity and to enrich the lives we touch.

Dedication

To my family and friends:

To my husband, Ed, who—although he claims to burn water—actually prepared many meals so I could pursue my dreams.

To my daughter, McKenzie, who loves movies as much as I do and who always cracks me up.

To my parents, Mom, Dad, and Pat, who taught me to believe you can do whatever you set your mind to.

To my sisters and brothers. We are always there for each other.

And to my best friend, Cornelia. You're the best, girlfriend.

Acknowledgments

A special thank you goes to Cornelia Gauger, the auditioner of fabrics, presser of seams, and typist extraordinaire. Thank you Roxanne Carter, Sue Lohse, and Frankie Schmitt for doing such a lovely job of quilting my creations. Thank you to my "family" at Martingale & Company, who always asked how my book was going and never showed how tired they must have been of me talking about it. Thanks to Steve Daley for creating my little doll icon. And finally, a special thank you to my benefactor, who funded the cost of the quilting—and then some.

Contents

Introduction

I have to confess up front that I have not been a quilter long. That is not to say I hadn't tried in the past. Like many of you, I imagine, I have a huge twenty-pound denim quilt—with king-size bed sheet as backing—that we use for picnics. But times have changed! With the fabulous selection of fabrics available today, along with the rotary cutter, mats, and sewing machines on the market, there is no stopping someone from creating a piece of fabric art.

I actually can blame my best friend for leading me down the quilter's path. She wanted to visit a quilt shop to look for a project. Within two hours, I had a book in hand and was on my way home to check the fabric stash. Two weeks later, the first quilt top was done, and that—as they say—was that. I was hooked.

Little did I know that the citrus fruit prints I chose for that quilt, left over from a splashy summer outfit I had made for my daughter, McKenzie, marked the beginning of a beautiful friendship. I discovered that I loved specialty (or conversation) prints and started collecting them. Fabrics with cherries, fruits, vegetables, hearts, cats, and babies; fabrics featuring baseball, football, apples, and horses. And especially Christmas fabrics in every color palette known to man. This was getting serious!

Then it happened. My husband, Ed, just had to ask what I was going to do with all of my "treasures." What!? What did he mean? And—for some odd reason—he looked at me sideways when I said it was okay just to look at and fondle them. He was heading for the commitment papers. I had to think fast.

It struck me. What *could* I do with them? How could I make each piece of fabulous conversation print stand out? I only had smaller-size pieces of fabric: fat quarters to one-yard cuts, and so many of one theme. Cutting these relatively large-scale prints into little bits would ruin the effect. They simply wouldn't do for a large quilt.

The bar quilt was the answer to my prayers. Every aspect of its format is perfect.

- The size of the quilt can be adjusted depending on the amount of fabric available. I can make it wider by adding more blocks to each row or make it longer by adding rows.

- Each row is a small quilt within itself. Using one theme fabric for each row showcases the fabric without requiring lots of yardage.

- All of the designs are "fat-quarter friendly." I can gather several fat-quarter pieces with the same theme and be on my way to a new design.

- Bar quilts stitch up quickly. The blocks are easy and show off the specialty fabrics perfectly. I can complete a row each day and by the end of the week have a finished quilt top.

- The bar-quilt format offers the opportunity to perfect piecing skills and try new blocks.

- I never get bored working on a bar quilt. Since each row is something new and different, it compels me to move to the next row. No need to make dozens of the same block.

- The bar quilt is extremely forgiving. It doesn't matter if seams don't match from one row to the next since each row is so different. If a row is too short, spacers make it seem like it was meant to be. Notice, for example, the Log Cabin Heart row in "Baby-Face Playtime" on page 17.

- It is the perfect quilt style for a serious fabric collector. It uses up a stash and is fabulous for those wonderful little fat-quarter packets I see in quilt shops. (Those charming ladies take the fabric-selection guessing game off my hands.)

- I can fit a bar quilt into any space and decor. For example, a vertical bar quilt fits perfectly into a tall, skinny wall space.

By now, I hope you have caught my enthusiasm for bar quilts. The joy of these quilts is that no two quilts are ever alike, and I learn something new from each and every one.

How to Use This Book

There are several ways to use this book. You may reproduce any (or all) of the ten quilt projects. Or, you may design your own quilt by combining rows and blocks taken from the projects or the Block Index provided on page 79.

The Block Index includes more than forty different blocks. It is organized by the size of the block, since I know that the block size may be more important than the block's "look" in fitting your quilt plan. Don't limit yourself to a specific block size all of the time. Stretch a row with spacing strips, or even use half blocks as I did in "Rugrats Rule, Adults Drool" (page 53) to make ends meet.

In addition to the Block Index, do check out the Bibliography on page 79. These books are a fabulous source for block designs and are great reference materials for your library.

You may also personalize any quilt by using the charted alphabet and numbers on page 80. Try an anniversary quilt with the name of the husband and wife and the marriage date. Incorporate a favorite motto, verse, or phrase you live by on the front of a quilt to give you daily inspiration. The fusible interfacing process (see page 11) is quick, easy, and gives you very accurate results without having to piece every single square.

Whichever approach you choose, please keep one thing in mind: stretch your imagination and your quilting sense. Let the fabric "speak" to you, and try to be flexible. Take that leap of faith, knowing that the quilt will look great when it is all put together.

Since I personally consider each row in a bar quilt to be a miniquilt, I give fabric requirements and instructions accordingly. In the materials list at the beginning of each project, I have included the total yardage requirements so you may use your existing fabric in the exact same manner as I have or purchase fabric especially for that particular quilt. However, I have also included the yardage required for each row in case you want to make some changes. This gives you the flexibility to use more scraps or fat quarters, or to incorporate more conversation fabrics.

As you look through the projects, you'll quickly notice my adorable, chubby little Matrushka doll icon. Not only is she sweet, but she tells you how many fat quarters to use in each project.

I love fat quarters. At first I didn't understand them. Why anyone would want to use an 18" x 22" piece of fabric instead of the standard ¼-yard cut was beyond me. Now I know they have more flexibility than a standard ¼-yard cut, and I use them all the time. They expand a fabric stash without breaking the bank and are great for accompanying the conversation prints I use so often. A fat-quarter packet of six or more fabrics makes a great starting point for a bar quilt. The fabrics coordinate nicely, and a few extra fabrics in larger pieces are all that is needed to complete the ensemble.

Finally, you'll notice that I have sprinkled hints and suggestions throughout the book. There is one, however, that I would like to share up front. The biggest lesson I learned from bar-quilt construction is never to join the rows together until all of the rows are complete. Even if you are making one of the ten projects in this book, your quilt may look better if you switch the rows around, adding or eliminating sashing if necessary. Lay all the rows out on your design surface (for me, that would be my living room floor!) and play with the layout before you start sewing the completed rows together. Some rows will look great next to each other, some will need small pieced joining rows to tie them together visually, and some will need solid-colored fabric to frame them. "Summers in Walla Walla" on page 73 and "Rugrats Rule, Adults Drool" on page 53 are both great examples of the "wait 'til the rows are finished" concept. The top three rows of "Summers in

6

Walla Walla" worked okay next to each other, but on the lower part of the quilt I needed to add the pieced sashing to visually coordinate the row above and below the sashing. "Rugrats Rule, Adults Drool," on the other hand, needed solid-colored sashing between rows because the rows were so busy and bright, they could not be joined without my eyes going crossed!

What this all boils down to is this: have fun and enjoy using theme, conversation, and specialty fabrics with wild and reckless abandon.

Quiltmaking Basics

Fabric

Select high-quality, 100 percent–cotton fabrics. They hold their shape well and are easy to handle. Cottons are also very forgiving, they are great for easing pieces together, and they naturally cling together as you piece. Cotton blends can be more difficult to stitch and press. Sometimes, however, a cotton blend is worth a little extra effort if it is the perfect fabric for your quilt.

Yardage requirements are provided for all projects in this book and are based on 42" of usable fabric after preshrinking.

Preshrink all fabric to test for colorfastness and remove excess dye. Wash dark and light colors separately so that dark colors do not run onto light fabrics. Some fabrics may require several rinses to eliminate excess dyes. Press fabrics so that you can cut pieces accurately.

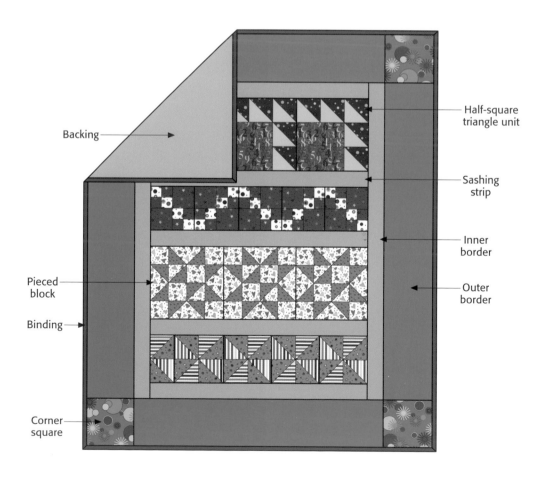

Backing

Half-square triangle unit

Sashing strip

Inner border

Pieced block

Outer border

Binding

Corner square

Anatomy of a Quilt

For those of you who are new to quilting, take a moment to review the different parts that make up a quilt (see page 6). I refer to sashing, inner and outer borders, corner blocks, and the like throughout the directions for the projects, and I don't want you to stumble when you are on a quiltmaking roll.

Supplies

Sewing machine: To machine piece, you'll need a sewing machine that has a good straight stitch. You'll also need a walking foot or darning foot if you plan to machine quilt. Take a moment to clean and oil your machine. In fact, get into the practice of cleaning your machine before beginning any project. Cotton is a great fiber, but it does create lint under the feed dogs that can interfere with the smooth running of your sewing machine.

Rotary-cutting tools: You will need a rotary cutter, cutting mat, and clear acrylic rulers in a variety of sizes, including 6" x 24" and 12" x 12".

Thread: Use a good-quality, all-purpose cotton or cotton-covered polyester thread. Choose a neutral color thread that won't show through when piecing light and dark fabrics together. Gray is a good choice.

Needles: For machine piecing, a size 10/70 or 12/80 works well for most cottons. For hand appliqué, size 10 (fine) to size 12 (very fine) needles work well; for hand quilting, use short, sturdy needles called "betweens."

Pins: Long, fine "quilter's pins" with glass or plastic heads are easy to handle.

Scissors: Use your best scissors to cut fabric only. Use an older pair of scissors to cut paper, cardboard, and template plastic. Small, 4" scissors with sharp points are handy for clipping thread.

Template plastic: Use clear or frosted plastic (available at quilt shops) to make durable, accurate templates.

Seam ripper: Use this tool to remove stitches from incorrectly sewn seams.

Marking tools: Use a sharp No. 2 pencil or fine-lead mechanical pencil on lighter-colored fabrics, and a silver or yellow marking pencil on darker fabrics. Chalk pencils or chalk-wheel markers also make clear marks on fabric. Be sure to test your pencil or chalk to make sure you can remove the marks easily.

Iron and ironing surface: A small craft iron set up near your sewing machine gives you quick access for pressing blocks as you stitch. Use a standard steam iron for pressing rows and larger sections of the quilt.

Fusible interfacing: Lightweight fusible interfacing with a preprinted gridded pattern is available from a variety of suppliers, including your local quilt shop or fabric store. You'll need it for two of the quilts in this book: "Just a Big City Girl!" (page 30) and "Batter Up!" (page 23).

Cutting

ROTARY CUTTING

All blocks are designed for easy rotary cutting and quick piecing, and measurements include standard ¼"-wide seam allowances. For those unfamiliar with rotary cutting, a brief introduction is provided below. For more detailed information, see Donna Thomas's *Shortcuts: A Concise Guide to Rotary Cutting* (That Patchwork Place, 1999).

8

1. Fold the fabric and match selvages, aligning the crosswise and lengthwise grains as much as possible. Place the folded edge closest to you on the cutting mat. Align a square ruler along the folded edge of the fabric. Then place a long, straight ruler to the left of the square ruler, just covering the uneven raw edges of the left side of the fabric.

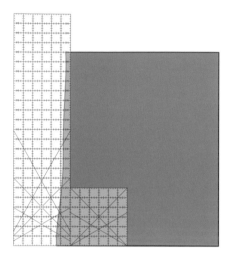

Remove the square ruler and cut along the right edge of the long ruler, rolling the rotary cutter away from you. Discard this strip. (Reverse this procedure if you are left-handed.)

2. To cut strips, align the required measurement on the ruler with the newly cut edge of the fabric. For example, to cut a 3"-wide strip, place the 3" ruler mark on the edge of the fabric.

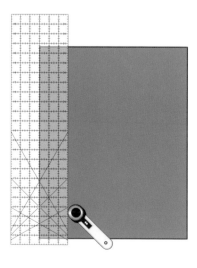

3. To cut squares, cut strips in the required widths. Trim away the selvage ends of the strip. Align the required measurement on the ruler with the left edge of the strip and cut a square. Continue cutting squares until you have the number you need.

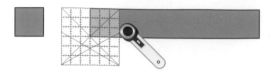

FUSSY CUTTING

Several projects in this book refer to "fussy cutting" those wonderful specialty fabrics. Fussy cutting is easy and gives you the opportunity to focus on a particular motif within the print of a fabric.

1. Determine the cut size of the shape within the block that you wish to feature the fussy-cut specialty print. Remember to include seam allowances if needed.

2. Use one of your rulers to frame the focus area on the fabric. You may trace this area with a pencil before cutting the piece from the fabric, or you may simply cut it out with the rotary cutter and ruler. More than likely the cut edges will not be on the grain of the fabric, so take care not to distort the piece as you stitch it into your block.

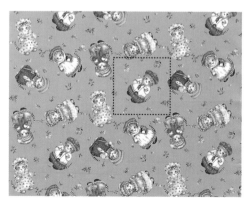

Cutting specific designs from fabric requires
extra yardage. Plan your cuts carefully.

HALF-SQUARE TRIANGLES

Make half-square triangles by cutting a square in half on the diagonal. The triangle's short sides are on the straight grain of the fabric.

1. Cut squares, using the finished measurement of the triangle's short sides, plus ⅞" for the seam allowances.
2. Stack the squares and cut once diagonally, corner to corner. Each square yields 2 triangles.

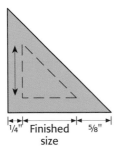
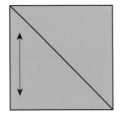

¼" Finished size ⅝"

¼" + ⅝" = ⅞"

QUARTER-SQUARE TRIANGLES

Make quarter-square triangles by cutting a square on both diagonals. The triangle's long side is on the straight grain of the fabric.

1. Cut squares, using the finished measurement of the triangle's long side, plus 1¼" for the seam allowances.
2. Stack the squares and cut twice diagonally, from corner to corner. Each square yields 4 triangles.

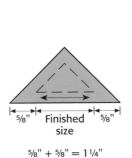
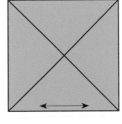

⅝" Finished size ⅝"

⅝" + ⅝" = 1¼"

Machine Piecing

The most important thing to remember about machine piecing is to maintain a consistent ¼"-wide seam allowance. Otherwise, the quilt block will not be the desired finished size. If that happens, the size of everything else in the quilt is affected, including alternate blocks, sashing, and borders. Measurements for all components of each quilt are based on blocks that finish accurately to the desired size, plus ¼" on each edge for seam allowances.

Take the time to establish an exact ¼"-wide seam guide on your machine. Some machines have a special foot that measures exactly ¼" from the center needle position to the edge of the foot. This feature allows you to use the edge of the presser foot to guide the fabric for a perfect ¼"-wide seam allowance.

If your machine doesn't have such a foot, create a seam guide by placing the edge of a piece of tape, moleskin, or a magnetic seam guide ¼" away from the needle.

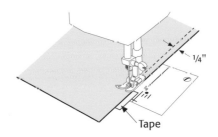

¼"

Tape

CHAIN PIECING

Chain piecing is an efficient, time-saving system.

1. Sew the first pair of pieces from cut edge to cut edge, using 12 stitches per inch. At the end of the seam, stop sewing, but do not cut the thread.
2. Feed the next pair of pieces under the presser foot, as close as possible to the first pair. Continue feeding pieces through the machine without cutting the threads in between. There is no need to backstitch, since each seam will be crossed and held by another seam.

10

3. When all pieces have been sewn, remove the chain from the machine and clip the threads between the pieces.

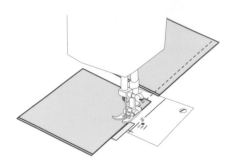

STRATA (STRIP) PIECING

Fabric strata is the name I use for the new "fabric" that is created by sewing two or more strips of fabric together to create a single fabric panel. Seams are pressed carefully, and the strata are cut apart into identical segments that work perfectly when you must piece a series of identical blocks. The technique is easy, accurate, and a real time-saver because it eliminates the cutting and restitching of lots of individual squares or rectangles.

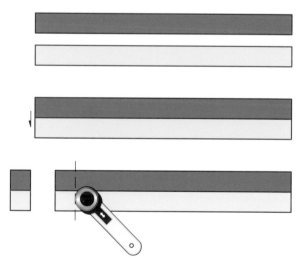

EASING

If two pieces that will be sewn together are slightly different in size (less than ⅛"), pin the places where the two pieces should match. Next pin the middle, if necessary, to distribute the excess fabric evenly. Sew the seam with the longer piece on the bottom, next to the feed dogs. The feed dogs will help ease the two pieces together.

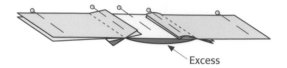

Excess

PRESSING

Before pressing, make sure the iron face is clean. Synthetic fabrics can leave a residue that bonds permanently to cotton, leaving a hard black mark on the surface of the fabric.

The traditional rule in quiltmaking is to press seams to one side, toward the darker color wherever possible. Press the seam flat from the wrong side first, and then press the seam in the desired direction from the right side. Press carefully to avoid distorting the shapes. Use an up and down motion and avoid sliding the iron back and forth over a block or row. Be particularly careful when pressing bias seams or edges. I usually use a dry iron for pressing bias seams and steam for straight-grain seams.

When joining two seamed units, plan ahead and press the seam allowances in opposite directions as shown. This reduces bulk and makes it easier to match seam lines. Where two seams meet, the seam allowances will butt against each other, making it easier to join units with perfectly matched seam intersections.

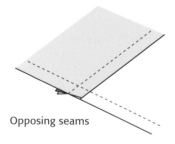

Opposing seams

PREPRINTED FUSIBLE INTERFACING

This is a quick, easy, and very accurate way to piece the small squares that form the rows of words in some of the quilts. Intersections match perfectly, and the interfacing adds strength to the row.

An alphabet and number chart is provided on page 79. Each letter and number measures five squares high. These charts may be used to draft the letters and numbers necessary for you to complete the projects in this book, but, if you prefer, you may use any charted alphabet.

Be sure to follow the directions suggested by the manufacturer for preprinted gridded interfacing (see page 7).

1. Draft the words and spaces required for your quilt as described in the project instructions. Allow one vertical row between each letter and three vertical rows between each word as you draft the row. In addition, add at least one horizontal row above and below the lettering to help frame the row (see figure below).

2. Count, and then cut the pieces required for the lettering and background to fill all the spaces. If your finished square measures 1", the cut square should measure 1½" (1" plus ¼" seam allowances).

3. Cut a piece of fusible interfacing to equal the overall unfinished size of your lettered pattern. In other words, if your finished pattern is 7" high, the interfacing should measure 10½" (7" x 1½").

4. Smooth the interfacing, web side up, on your ironing surface. Refer to the charted design, and beginning in the lower right-hand corner, place the squares of letter and background fabric on the webbing. Press them in place with a dry iron.

Tip By working on your ironing surface, you'll eliminate the need to move the interfacing topped with dozens of unfused fabric squares!

5. Starting at the right end, fold the first vertical row right sides together, and stitch from top to bottom, taking a scant ¼"-wide seam. Repeat for each vertical row.

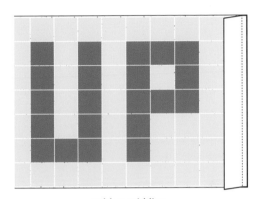

Fold at grid line.
Stitch scant ¼" seam.

6. Clip the seams at the square intersections to avoid bulk, and press seam allowances in opposite directions from row to row.

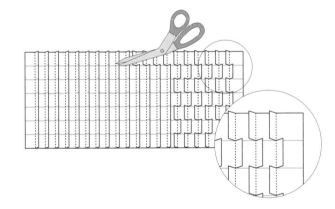

7. In the same manner, stitch and press each horizontal row.

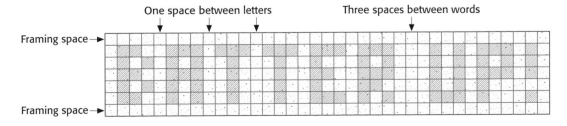

One space between letters   Three spaces between words

Framing space →

Framing space →

Adding Borders

12

For best results, do not cut border strips and sew them directly to the quilt sides without measuring first. The edges of a quilt often measure slightly longer than the distance through the quilt center, due to stretching during construction. Instead, measure the quilt top through the center in both directions to determine how long to cut border strips. This step ensures that the finished quilt will be as straight and as "square" as possible, without wavy edges.

Plain border strips are commonly cut along the crosswise grain and seamed where extra length is needed. Borders cut from the lengthwise grain of fabric require extra yardage, but seaming the required length is then unnecessary.

STRAIGHT-CUT BORDERS

All of the quilts in this book are made with straight-cut borders.

1. Measure the length of the quilt top through the center. Cut border strips to that measurement, piecing as necessary. Mark the center of the quilt edges and the border strips. Pin the borders to the sides of the quilt top, matching the center marks and ends, and easing as necessary. Sew the border strips in place. Press seams toward the border.

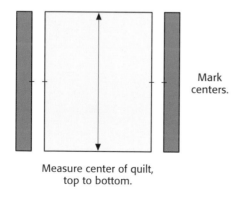

Measure center of quilt, top to bottom.

Mark centers.

2. Measure the width of the quilt top through the center, including the side borders just added. Cut border strips to that measurement, piecing as necessary. Mark the center of the quilt edges and the border strips. Pin the borders to the top and bottom edges of the quilt top, matching the center marks and ends and easing as necessary; stitch. Press seams toward the border.

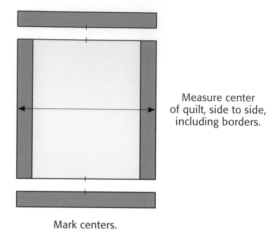

Measure center of quilt, side to side, including borders.

Mark centers.

BORDERS WITH CORNER SQUARES

1. Measure the width and length of the quilt top through the center. Cut border strips to those measurements, piecing as necessary.

2. Mark the center of the quilt edges and the border strips. Pin the side border strips to opposite sides of the quilt top, matching centers and ends, and easing as necessary. Sew the side border strips, and press seams toward the border.

3. Cut corner squares the required size; that is, the cut width of the border strips. Sew one corner square to each end of the remaining two border strips, and press seams toward the border strips. Pin the border strips to the top and bottom

edges of the quilt top. Match centers, seams between the border strip and corner square, and ends, easing as necessary; stitch. Press seams toward the border.

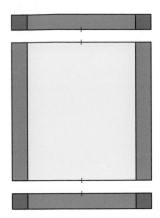

Quilting

MARKING THE QUILTING LINES

Whether or not to mark the quilting designs depends upon the type of quilting you will be doing. For hand quilting, marking is not necessary if you plan to quilt in-the-ditch or outline-quilt a uniform distance from seam lines. For more complex quilting designs, mark the quilt top before the quilt is layered with batting and backing. For machine quilting, marking is necessary if you need to follow a grid or a complex pattern. It is not necessary if you plan to quilt in-the-ditch, outline-quilt a uniform distance from seam lines, or free-motion quilt in a random pattern over the quilt surface or in selected areas.

Choose a marking tool that will be visible on your fabric, and test it on fabric scraps to be sure the marks can be removed easily. Masking tape can be used to mark straight quilting. Tape only small sections at a time and remove the tape when you stop at the end of the day. Otherwise, the sticky residue may be difficult to remove from the fabric.

LAYERING THE QUILT

The quilt "sandwich" consists of backing, batting, and the quilt top. Cut the quilt backing at least 4" larger than the quilt top all the way around. For large quilts, it is usually necessary to sew two or three lengths of fabric together to make a backing of the required size. Trim away the selvages before piecing the lengths together. Press seams open to make quilting easier.

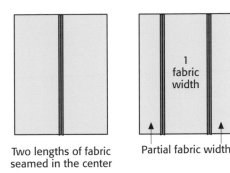

Two lengths of fabric seamed in the center

Partial fabric width

1 fabric width

Batting comes packaged in standard bed sizes, or it can be purchased by the yard. Several weights or thicknesses are available. Thick battings are fine for tied quilts and comforters; a thinner batting is better, however, if you intend to quilt by hand or machine.

To put it all together:

1. Spread the backing, wrong side up, on a flat, clean surface. Anchor it with pins or masking tape. Be careful not to stretch the backing out of shape.

2. Spread the batting over the backing, smoothing out any wrinkles.

3. Place the pressed quilt top, right side up, on top of the batting. Smooth out any wrinkles and make sure the quilt-top edges are parallel to the edges of the backing.

14

4. Starting in the center, baste with needle and thread, working diagonally to each corner. Continue basting in a grid of horizontal and vertical lines 6" to 8" apart. Finish by basting around the edges.

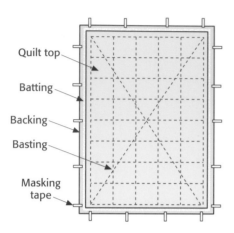

Quilt top
Batting
Backing
Basting
Masking tape

NOTE: For machine quilting, you may baste the layers with No. 2 rustproof safety pins. Place pins about 6" to 8" apart, away from the areas you intend to quilt.

HAND QUILTING

To quilt by hand, you will need short, sturdy needles (called "betweens"), quilting thread, and a thimble to fit the middle finger of your sewing hand. Most quilters also use a frame or hoop to support their work. Use the smallest needle you can comfortably handle; the finer the needle, the smaller your stitches will be.

1. Thread your needle with a single strand of quilting thread about 18" long. Make a small knot and insert the needle in the top layer about 1" from the place where you want to start stitching. Pull the needle out at the point where quilting will begin. Gently pull the thread until the knot pops through the fabric and into the batting.

2. Take small, evenly spaced stitches through all three quilt layers. Rock the needle up and down through all layers, until you have three or four stitches on the needle. Place your other hand

underneath the quilt so you can feel the needle point with the tip of your finger when a stitch is taken.

3. To end a line of quilting, make a small knot close to the last stitch. Backstitch, running the thread a needle's length through the batting. Gently pull the thread until the knot pops into the batting; clip the thread at the quilt's surface.

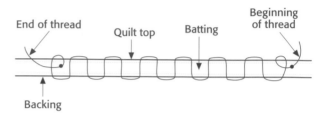

End of thread   Quilt top   Batting   Beginning of thread

Backing

MACHINE QUILTING

Machine quilting is suitable for all types of quilts, from crib to full-size bed quilts. With machine quilting, you can quickly complete quilts that might otherwise languish on the shelves.

For straight-line quilting, it is extremely helpful to have a walking foot to help feed the quilt layers through the machine without shifting or puckering. Some machines have a built-in walking foot; other machines require a separate attachment.

Walking Foot

Quilting in-the-Ditch   Outline Quilting

For free-motion quilting, you'll need a darning foot and the ability to drop the feed dogs on your machine. With free-motion quilting, you do not turn the fabric under the needle, but instead guide the fabric in the direction of the design. Use free-motion quilting to outline-quilt a fabric motif or to create stippling or other curved designs.

Darning Foot

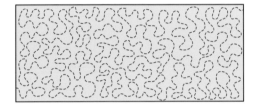

Free-Motion Quilting

Finishing

BINDING

Bindings can be made from straight-grain or bias-grain strips of fabric. For a straight-grain, French double-fold binding, cut strips 2½" wide across the width of the fabric. You will need enough strips to go around the perimeter of the quilt, plus 10" for seams and the corners in a mitered fold.

1. Join strips at right angles, right sides together, and stitch across the corner as shown to make one long length of binding. Trim excess fabric and press the seams open.

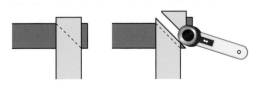

Joining Straight-Cut Strips

2. Fold the strip in half lengthwise, wrong sides together, and press. Turn under ¼" at a 45-degree angle at one end of the strip and press. Turning the end under at an angle distributes the bulk so you won't have a lump where the two ends of the binding meet.

Fold line

3. Trim the batting and backing even with the quilt top. If you plan to add a sleeve, do so now before attaching the binding (see right).

4. Starting on one side of the quilt and using a ⅜"-wide seam allowance, stitch the binding to the quilt, keeping the raw edges even with the quilt-top edge. End the stitching ⅜" from the corner of the quilt and backstitch. Clip the thread.

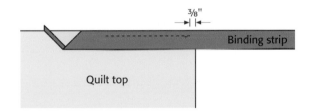

⅜"

Binding strip

Quilt top

5. Turn the quilt so that you'll be stitching down the next side. Fold the binding up, away from the quilt, then back down onto itself, parallel with the edge of the quilt top. Begin stitching at the edge, backstitching to secure. Repeat on the remaining edges and corners of the quilt.

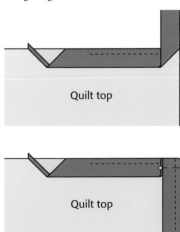

Quilt top

Quilt top

6. When you reach the beginning of the binding, overlap the beginning stitches by 1" and cut away any excess binding, trimming the end at a 45-degree angle. Tuck the end of the binding into the fold and finish the seam.

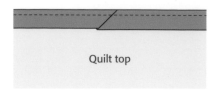

Quilt top

7. Fold the binding over the raw edges of the quilt to the back, with the folded edge covering the row of machine stitching, and blindstitch in place. A miter will form at each corner. Blindstitch the mitered corners.

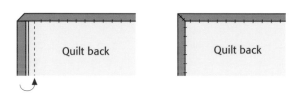

Quilt back   Quilt back

ADDING A SLEEVE

If you plan to display your finished quilt on the wall, be sure to add a hanging sleeve to hold the rod.

1. Using leftover fabric from the quilt (or a piece of muslin), cut a strip 6" to 8" wide and 1" shorter than the width of the quilt's top edge. Fold the ends under ½", then ½" again; stitch.

2. Fold the fabric strip in half lengthwise, wrong sides together, and baste the raw edges to the top edge of the quilt back. The top edge of the sleeve will be secured when the binding is sewn on.

Baste sleeve to top edge of quilt.

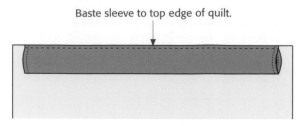

3. Finish the sleeve after the binding has been attached by blindstitching the bottom of the sleeve in place. Push the bottom edge of the sleeve up just a bit. This provides a little give so the hanging rod does not put strain on the quilt itself.

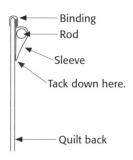

Binding
Rod
Sleeve
Tack down here.

Quilt back

SIGNING YOUR QUILT

Be sure to sign and date your quilt. Future generations will be interested to know more than just who made it and when. Labels can be as elaborate or as simple as you desire. The information can be handwritten, typed, or embroidered. Be sure to include the name of the quilt, your name, your city and state, the date, the name of the recipient if it is a gift, and any other interesting or important information about the quilt.

Baby-Face Playtime

Terry Martin, 1999, Snohomish, Washington, 47½" x 51½"; machine quilted by Dizzy Stitches.

▶ As SWEET AS THIS QUILT LOOKS, it was one of my biggest challenges. I had barely more than a yard of the cute baby print. The motifs were large and spread apart, making it difficult to work into blocks with small pieces. Also, since this fabric, with its "vintage" babies, was so specialized, I wondered how to choose accompanying fabric. I tried the time-honored approach of laying it out on the dining room table and passing by several times a day. After checking my fabric stash several times, I added the tone-on-tone fabrics. These were colors that I wanted to highlight from the baby print, but I still felt there was something missing from the combination. Back I went to the fabric stash. Hm-m-m . . . the heart fabric coordinated colorwise and added some additional jazzy colors. But the print was very "now," very "wow." I still wondered, would it work? Taking that quilting "leap of faith," I started cutting. The heart fabric for the heart block? Too perfect! How does it look next to the baby print? You be the judge. Personally, I believe mixing different theme fabrics added punch to this bar quilt without compromising the integrity of the main fabric selection.

Materials (42"-wide fabric)

N O T E : Yardages listed are for the entire quilt as shown in the color photo on page 17. Instructions for each row indicate the yardage required for that row only.

⅜ yd. Fabric A (heart print) for Rows 1, 3, and 6

¼ yd. Fabric B (white-on-white print) for sashing and Rows 1, 3, and 4

1¼ yds. Fabric C (baby print) for border and Rows 2 and 5

⅞ yd. Fabric D (red tone-on-tone print) for sashing, binding, and Rows 1, 2, 4, and 6

½ yd. Fabric E (gold tone-on-tone print) for sashing and Rows 1, 3, 4, and 5

⅜ yd. Fabric F (blue tone-on-tone print) for Rows 1, 3, 4, and 6

⅜ yd. Fabric G (green tone-on-tone print) for Rows 1, 4, 5, and 6

3 yds. fabric for backing

50" x 55" piece of batting

Cutting Sashing, Borders, and Binding

All cutting measurements include ¼"-wide seam allowances.

From *each* of Fabrics B and D, cut:

1 strip, 1½" x 36½", for sashing

From Fabric E, cut:

2 strips, each 1½" x 36½", for sashing

From Fabric C, cut:

5 strips, each 6" x 42", for border

From Fabric D, cut:

5 strips, each 2½" x 42", for binding

Cutting and Piecing the Rows

Refer to "Quiltmaking Basics" on page 6 for general construction techniques and to the assembly diagram on page 22 for guidance as you piece each row.

All cutting measurements include ¼"-wide seam allowances.

Row 1

Finished Unit Size: 3" x 3¾"

⅛ yd. Fabric B; scraps of Fabrics D, E, F, and G; ¼ yd. Fabric A

CUTTING

From Fabric B, cut:

24 squares, each 1½" x 1½"

From Fabrics D, E, F, and G scraps, cut a *total* of:

12 rectangles, each 1½" x 2¼"

From Fabric A, cut:

12 rectangles, each 2½" x 4¼"

ASSEMBLY

NOTE: This row has been modified *slightly* from Row 1 as shown in the photo on page 17. Use the diagram on page 22 for reference as needed.

1. With right sides together, sew a 1½" Fabric B square to both short ends of one 1½" x 2¼" Fabric D, E, F, or G rectangle. Press seams toward the rectangles. Make 12.

2. Sew a unit from step 1 to the right edge of a 2½" x 4¼" Fabric A rectangle. Press seams toward the Fabric A rectangles. Make 12.

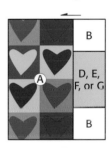

Make 12.

3. Join the 12 units in a horizontal row, randomly mixing the colors. Press seams to one side.

Row 2

Block Name: X-quisite

Finished Block Size: 6"

1 fat quarter *each* of Fabrics C and D

CUTTING

From Fabric C, cut:

6 squares, each 6½" x 6½"

From Fabric D, cut:

12 squares, each 3½" x 3½"

ASSEMBLY

1. Draw a diagonal line from corner to corner on the back side of each 3½" Fabric D square.

2. With right sides together, position and pin a Fabric D square in 2 opposite corners of each 6½" Fabric C square as shown. Sew directly on the marked lines.

3. Trim, leaving a ¼"-wide seam allowance. Press seams toward the corner triangles. Make 6.

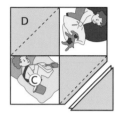

Make 6.

4. Join the 6 blocks in a horizontal row. Press seams to one side.

Row 3

Block Name: Log Cabin Heart

Finished Block Size: 4¼"

⅛ yd. *each* of Fabrics A and E; scraps of Fabric B; 1 fat quarter Fabric F

CUTTING

From Fabric A, cut:

8 squares, each 2" x 2"

8 rectangles, each 2" x 3½"

From Fabric B, cut:

8 squares, each 2" x 2"

From Fabric E, cut:

8 squares, each 3" x 3"; cut squares once diagonally to make 16 triangles

From Fabric F, cut:

8 squares, each 3" x 3"; cut squares once diagonally to make 16 triangles

2 rectangles, each 1½" x 4¾"

2 strips, each 1½" x 36½"

20

ASSEMBLY

1. With right sides together, sew a 2" Fabric A and Fabric B square together. Press seams toward the Fabric A squares. Make 8.

2. Sew one 2" x 3½" Fabric A rectangle to a unit from step 1, taking care to position the squares as shown. Press seams toward the Fabric A rectangle. Make 8.

3. Sew a Fabric E triangle to the upper left and lower right sides of each unit from step 2 as shown. Press seams toward the triangles. Repeat to sew a Fabric F triangle to the upper right and lower left sides of each unit; press.

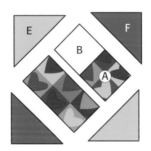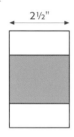

Make 8.

4. Join the 8 blocks in a horizontal row, beginning and ending the row with a 1½" x 4¾" Fabric F rectangle. Press seams to one side.

5. With right sides together, and matching centers and ends, pin and sew a 1½" x 36½" Fabric F strip to the top and bottom of the row. Press seams toward the strips.

Row 4

Block Name: Puss in the Corner
Finished Unit Size: 3" x 4"
¼ yd. Fabric B; ⅛ yd. *each* of Fabrics D, E, F, and G

CUTTING

From Fabric B, cut:
    2 strips, each 2½" x 10"
    8 strips, each 1½" x 8½"
From *each* of Fabrics D, E, F, and G, cut:
    1 strip, 2½" x 8½"
    1 strip, 1½" x 10"

ASSEMBLY

1. With right sides together and long raw edges aligned, sew one 2½" x 8½" Fabric D strip between two 1½" x 8½" Fabric B strips to make a 4½" x 8½" strip set. Press seams away from the Fabric B strips.

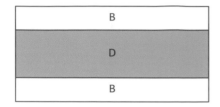

Make 1 strip set.

2. Crosscut the strip set into three 2½" segments.

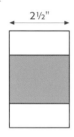

Cut 3.

3. Repeat steps 1 and 2 using the 2½" x 8½" Fabric E, F, and G strips in place of Fabric D.

4. With right sides together and long raw edges aligned, sew one 2½" x 10" Fabric B strip between two randomly chosen 1½" x 10" Fabric D, E, F, and G strips. Press seams away from the Fabric B strips. You'll have 2 strip sets, each measuring 4½" x 10".

D, E, F, or G
B
D, E, F, or G

Make 2 strip sets.

5. Crosscut the strip sets into a total of twelve 1½" segments.

Cut 12.

6. Sew a segment from step 2 or step 3 to a randomly chosen segment from step 5. Press seams in one direction. Make 12.

7. Randomly join the 12 units in a horizontal row. Press seams to one side.

Row 5

Block Name: Cotton Reel
Finished Block Size: 8"
1 fat quarter *each* of Fabrics C, E, and G

CUTTING

From *each* of Fabrics E and G, cut:

5 squares, each 4⅞" x 4⅞"; cut squares once diagonally to make 10 triangles
From Fabric C, cut:

9 squares, each 4½" x 4½"

ASSEMBLY

1. Sew a Fabric E and Fabric G triangle together along the long diagonal edge. Press seams toward the Fabric G triangle. Make 9. (You'll have 1 triangle of each color left over. Set aside for another project.)

2. Sew each unit from step 1 to a 4½" Fabric C square, taking care to position the triangles as shown. Press seams toward the Fabric C squares. Make 9.

3. Sew units from step 2 in pairs as shown. Press seams in opposite directions from block to block. Make 4.

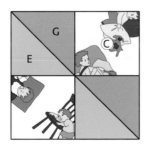

Make 4.

4. Join the 4 blocks in a horizontal row. End the row with the remaining unit from step 2. Press seams to one side.

Row 6

Block Name: Rail Fence
Finished Block Size: 8"
⅛ yd. *each* of Fabrics A, D, F, and G

CUTTING

From *each* of Fabrics A, D, F, and G, cut:

2 strips, each 1½" x 42"

ASSEMBLY

1. With right sides together and long raw edges aligned, sew 1½" x 42" strips together in the following order to make a 4½" x 42" strip set: 1 each of Fabric A, Fabric F, Fabric D, and Fabric G. Press seams in one direction. Make 2 strip sets.

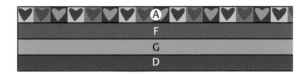

Make 2 strip sets.

2. Crosscut the strip sets into a total of eighteen 4½" segments.

Cut 18.

3. Sew segments from step 2 in pairs, taking care to position strips as shown. Press seams toward the Fabric A strip. Make 9.

Make 9.

4. Join the 9 units in a horizontal row, taking care to position them properly. Press seams to one side.

22

QUILT ASSEMBLY

Refer to the assembly diagram below. Arrange Rows 1–6 and the four 1½" x 36½" sashing strips as shown. With right sides together, and matching centers and ends, pin and sew the rows and sashing together. Press seams toward the sashing strips.

ADDING THE BORDERS

Refer to "Adding Borders" on page 12.

Sew the 6" x 42" Fabric C border strips together, end to end, to make a continuous 6"-wide strip. Cut the border strips from this 6"-wide strip; sew the strips first to the sides, then to the top and bottom. Press seams toward borders.

FINISHING

Refer to "Quilting" and "Finishing" on pages 13–16.

1. Divide the backing fabric crosswise into 2 equal panels of approximately 54" each. Remove the selvages and join the pieces to make a single, large backing panel.

2. Center and layer the quilt top and the batting over the backing; baste.

3. Quilt as desired.

4. Trim the batting and backing even with the edges of the quilt top. Use the 2½" x 42" Fabric D strips to make the binding; sew the binding to the quilt.

5. Make and attach a label to your quilt.

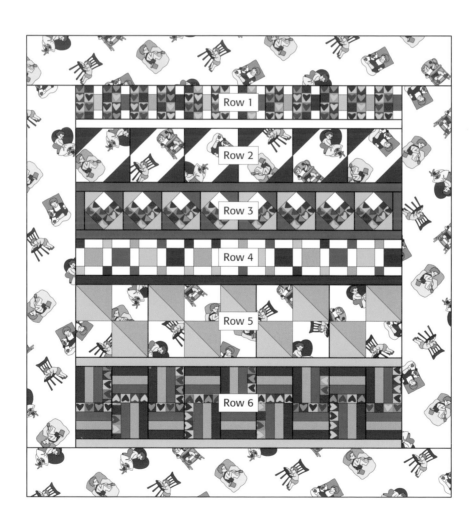

Batter Up!

Terry Martin, 1999, Snohomish, Washington, 49½" x 68½"; machine quilted by Dizzy Stitches.

24

▶ IT IS MY PHILOSOPHY THAT FOR EVERY twenty projects you make for yourself, friends, and family, one of those should be for your husband. This gesture should be for no reason at all, just "because."

My husband, Ed, is the greatest, and the fabric-shop owners love him. He holds my pile of bolts and chats enthusiastically about fabric and quilting with customers. He is very proud of my work, and every time I drag him to a quilt show, he comes home determined to take a sewing class.

He also loves baseball. Although it's not in the colors of his favorite team (the Seattle Mariners), he has claimed this quilt as his own.

I had lots of fun designing this quilt with baseball diamonds in mind. The blocks came together with simple sashing, so the fabric and design could take center stage.

Trying to stay within a three-color scheme of red, black, and white was a challenge! It was nice to have bits of other colors in the key fabrics to soften the bold color palette. What do you think of the extra-large Northwind blocks on the bottom row? I think they add a solid anchor to the quilt, and—the best part—I only had to make three!

Materials (42"-wide fabric)

NOTE: Yardages listed are for the entire quilt as shown in the color photo on page 23. Instructions for each row indicate the yardage required for that row only.

1 fat quarter Fabric A (red print) for Row 1

1 fat quarter Fabric B (red check) for Rows 1 and 5

1 fat quarter Fabric C (black and cream print) for Row 1

1⅛ yds. Fabric D (baseball print) for binding and Rows 2 and 5

1⅜ yds. Fabric E (red tone-on-tone print) for sashing and Rows 2, 3, 4, and 6

⅓ yd. Fabric F (bat print) for Row 3

¼ yd. Fabric G (black solid) for Rows 3 and 5

⅝ yd. Fabric H (mitt print) for Rows 4 and 6

1 fat quarter Fabric I (white print) for Row 4

1⅛ yds. Fabric J (large-scale theme print) for border

11" x 56" (minimum) piece of gridded lightweight fusible interfacing

3 yds. fabric for backing

53" x 74" piece of batting

Cutting Sashing, Borders, and Binding

All cutting measurements include ¼"-wide seam allowances.

From Fabric E, cut:

7 strips, each 1½" x 36½", for horizontal sashing

4 strips, each 1½" x 42", for vertical sashing

From Fabric J, cut:

6 strips, each 6" x 42", for border

From Fabric D, cut:

6 strips, each 2½" x 42", for binding

Cutting and Piecing the Rows

Refer to "Quiltmaking Basics" on page 6 for general construction techniques and to the assembly diagram on page 29 for guidance as you piece each row.

Row 2 features words that are pieced using gridded fusible interfacing (page 11) and the Alphabet/Number Chart on page 79.

All cutting measurements include ¼"-wide seam allowances.

Row 1

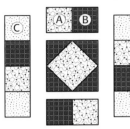

Block Name: Susannah
Finished Block Size: 8"
1 fat quarter *each* of Fabrics A, B, and C

CUTTING

From Fabric A, cut:
> 4 squares, each 3⅜" x 3⅜"
> 18 squares, each 2½" x 2½"

From Fabric B, cut:
> 8 squares, each 2⅞" x 2⅞"; cut squares once diagonally to make 16 triangles
> 18 squares, each 2½" x 2½"

From Fabric C, cut:
> 20 squares, each 2½" x 2½"

ASSEMBLY

1. With right sides together, sew the long side of a Fabric B triangle to 2 opposite sides of each 3⅜" Fabric A square. Press seams toward the triangles. Repeat to sew a Fabric B triangle to the remaining sides of the Fabric A square. Press seams toward the triangles.

2. Sew a 2½" Fabric A square and a Fabric B square together. Press seams toward the Fabric A squares. Make 18.

3. Sew a unit from step 2 to the top and bottom of each unit from step 1, taking care to position the squares as shown. Press seams away from the center unit.

4. Sew a 2½" Fabric C square to both short ends of each remaining unit from step 2. Press seams away from the Fabric C squares.

5. Sew a unit from step 4 to the sides of each unit from step 3. Press seams in opposite directions from block to block. Make 4 blocks. You'll have 2 units from step 4 left.

Make 4.

6. Join the 4 blocks in a horizontal row. Begin and end the row with the remaining 2 units from step 4. Press seams to one side.

Row 2

Row Name: Batter Up!
Finished Row Size: 36" x 7"
1 fat quarter Fabric E; ⅓ yd. Fabric D; 11" x 56" piece (minimum) of gridded lightweight fusible interfacing

CUTTING

From Fabric E, cut:
> 83 squares, each 1½" x 1½"

From Fabric D, cut:
> 176 squares, each 1½" x 1½"

ASSEMBLY

Refer to "Preprinted Fusible Interfacing" on page 11. The grid for this row is marked 37 squares across and 7 squares down to allow for extra uptake and bulk in the many vertical seams. The *finished* panel should measure 36" across.

1. Using preprinted gridded fusible interfacing, lay the fusible interfacing, fusible side up, on a surface that can be ironed with a dry iron.

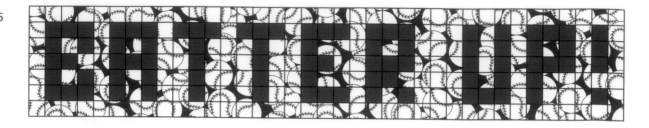

2. Refer to the diagram above, and beginning in the lower right-hand corner, place the 1½" Fabric D and E squares on the webbing to fill in the lettering and background. See the Alphabet/Number chart on page 79 if you wish to use a different phrase in this row.

3. Follow the manufacturer's instructions to fuse the squares to the interfacing.

4. Sew the vertical and horizontal seam lines.

Row 3

Block Name: Baseball Diamond
Finished Block Size: 9"
⅛ yd. Fabric E; ⅓ yd. Fabric F; scraps of Fabric G

CUTTING

From Fabric E, cut:

16 rectangles, each 1¾" x 4⅜"

From Fabric F, cut:

8 squares, each 5⅜" x 5⅜"; cut squares once diagonally to make 16 triangles

4 squares, each 4⅜" x 4⅜"

From Fabric G, cut:

16 squares, each 1¾" x 1¾"

ASSEMBLY

1. With right sides together, sew a 1¾" x 4⅜" Fabric E rectangle to 2 opposite sides of each 4⅜" Fabric F square. Press seams toward the rectangles. Make 4.

2. Sew a 1¾" Fabric G square to both short ends of each remaining 1¾" x 4⅜" Fabric E rectangle. Press seams toward the rectangles. Make 8.

3. Sew each unit from step 1 between 2 units from step 2. Press seams away from the center unit.

4. Sew a Fabric F triangle to 2 opposite sides of each unit from step 3. Press seams toward the triangles. Repeat to sew a Fabric F triangle to the remaining 2 sides of each unit; press.

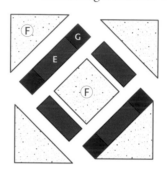
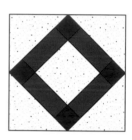

Make 4.

5. Join the 4 blocks in a horizontal row. Press seams to one side.

Row 4

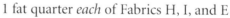

Block Name: Paper Pinwheels
Finished Block Size: 6"
1 fat quarter *each* of Fabrics H, I, and E

CUTTING

From Fabric H, cut:

6 squares, each 3½" x 3½"

12 squares, each 2⅜" x 2⅜"; cut squares once diagonally to make 24 triangles

From Fabric I, cut:

12 squares, each 2⅜" x 2⅜"; cut squares once diagonally to make 24 triangles

24 squares, each 2" x 2"

From Fabric E, cut:

24 squares, each 2" x 2"

ASSEMBLY

1. Sew a Fabric H and Fabric I triangle together along the long diagonal edge. Press seams toward Fabric H. Make 24.

2. Sew a 2" Fabric E square to each unit from step 1, taking care to position the triangles as shown. Press seams toward the Fabric E square. Make 24.

3. Sew a 3½" Fabric H square between 2 units from step 2 as shown. Press seams away from the center square. Make 6.

4. Sew a remaining unit from step 2 between two 2" Fabric I squares as shown. Press seams away from the Fabric I squares. Make 12.

5. Sew each unit from step 3 between 2 units from step 4 as shown. Press seams in opposite directions from block to block.

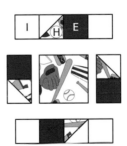 

Make 6.

6. Join the 6 blocks in a horizontal row. Press seams to one side.

Row 5

Block Name: Patience

Finished Block Size: 9"

¼ yd. Fabric D; ⅛ yd. *each* of Fabrics B and G

CUTTING

From Fabric D, cut:

2 strips, each 4" x 42"

From *each* of Fabrics B and G, cut:

1 strip, 1½" x 42"

8 rectangles, each 1½" x 5"

ASSEMBLY

1. With right sides together and long raw edges aligned, sew the 1½"-wide Fabric G strip to a 4" Fabric D strip to make a 5" x 42" strip set. Press seams toward the Fabric G strip.

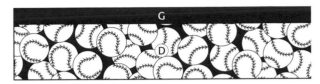

Make 1 strip set.

2. Crosscut the strip set from step 1 into eight 4" segments.

Cut 8.

3. Repeat steps 1 and 2, using the 1½"-wide Fabric B strip and the remaining 4" wide Fabric D strip. Press seams toward the Fabric B strip, and crosscut eight 4" segments.

4. Sew a 1½" x 5" Fabric G rectangle to a unit from step 2 as shown; press seams toward the Fabric G rectangle. Repeat to sew a 1½" x 5" Fabric B rectangle to a unit from step 3 as shown; press. Make 8 of each.

5. Using the units from step 4, sew a Fabric G unit to each Fabric B unit, taking care to position the units as shown. Press seams toward the Fabric G strip. Make 8.

6. Sew units from step 5 together in pairs, taking care to position the units as shown. Press seams in one direction. Make 4.

 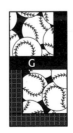 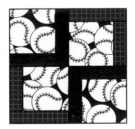

Make 4.

7. Join the 4 blocks in a horizontal row. Press seams to one side.

28

Row 6

Block Name: Northwind
Finished Block Size: 12"
½ yd. *each* of Fabrics E and H

CUTTING

From *each* of Fabrics E and H, cut:

2 squares, each 8⅞" x 8⅞"; cut squares once diagonally to make 4 triangles. You'll have 1 extra triangle of each fabric; set these aside for another project.

8 squares, each 4⅞" x 4⅞"; cut squares once diagonally to make 16 triangles. You'll have an extra triangle of each fabric; set these aside for another project.

ASSEMBLY

1. Sew a small Fabric E and Fabric H triangle together along the long diagonal edge. Press seams toward the Fabric E triangle. Make 9.

2. Sew a small Fabric H triangle to the right edge of a unit from step 1, taking care to position the triangles as shown. Press the seams toward the Fabric H triangle. Make 3.

Make 3.

3. Sew a unit from step 1 between a small Fabric H and Fabric E triangle as shown. Press seams away from the Fabric H triangle. Make 3.

Make 3.

4. Sew a small Fabric E triangle to the left edge of a unit from step 1. Press the seams toward the Fabric H triangle. Make 3.

Make 3.

5. Sew a unit from step 3 between a unit from step 2 and a unit from step 4, taking care to position and stagger the units as shown. Press seams in one direction. Make 3.

6. Sew a large Fabric E triangle to the lower right corner of each unit from step 5. Press seams toward the corner triangle. Repeat to sew a large Fabric H triangle to the upper left corner; press.

Make 3.

7. Join the 3 blocks in a horizontal row. Press seams to one side.

QUILT ASSEMBLY

1. Refer to the assembly diagram on page 29. Arrange Rows 1–6 and the 1½" x 36½" Fabric E sashing strips as shown. With right sides together, and matching centers and ends, pin and sew the rows and sashing together. Press seams toward the sashing strips.

2. Sew the 1½" x 42" sashing strips together in pairs. Measure the quilt through its vertical center, and cut the pieced sashing strips to this measurement. With right sides together, and matching centers and ends, pin and sew the trimmed sashing strips to the left and right sides of the quilt. Press the seams toward the sashing strips.

ADDING THE BORDERS

Refer to "Adding Borders" on page 12.

Sew the 6" x 42" Fabric J border strips together, end to end, to make a continuous 6"-wide strip. Cut the border strips from this 6"-wide strip; sew the strips first to the sides, then to the top and bottom.

FINISHING

Refer to "Quilting" and "Finishing" on pages 13–16.

1. Divide the backing fabric crosswise into 2 equal panels of approximately 54" each. Remove the selvages and join the pieces to make a single, large backing panel.

2. Position the backing so the seam runs horizontally. Center and layer the quilt top and the batting over the backing; baste.

3. Quilt as desired.

4. Trim the batting and backing even with the edges of the quilt top. Use the 2½" x 42" Fabric D strips to make the binding; sew the binding to the quilt.

5. Make and attach a label to your quilt.

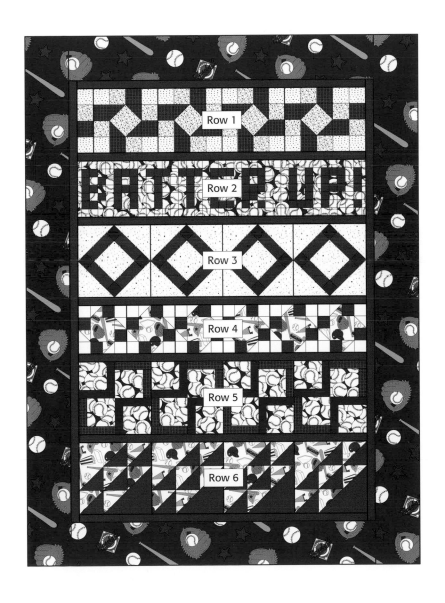

Just a Big City Girl!

Terry Martin, 1999, Snohomish, Washington, 36½" x 74"; machine quilted by Dizzy Stitches.

IT REALLY IS AMAZING WHAT FABRIC manufacturers can do these days! The complexity of print, the variety of color, and the use of metallics just fascinate me.

The cityscape fabric used in this quilt is a perfect example. I liked its dark sparkle and edginess, and I've visited all of the cities it depicts. From the moment I spied it, I knew I must own some. Of course, I purchased just one yard (will I ever learn?); thus, a skinny quilt.

I kept all of the colors on the cool side. Even the red has some gray in it, and the yellow is an acid hue. The Attic Window blocks give a "looking out from within" perspective to the skyline.

This quilt is very fast and easy. Use any fabric that features a horizontal motif, vary the width of the panels, and you will end up with a striking wall quilt, great for a high wall in a staircase or entryway.

Materials (42"-wide fabric)

NOTE: Yardages listed are for the entire quilt as shown in the color photo opposite. Instructions for each row indicate the yardage required for that row only.

1 ½ yds. Fabric A (cityscape panel print) for Rows 1, 3, 6, 8, 10, and 12*

¼ yd. Fabric B (red print) for Row 2

¼ yd. Fabric C (gray print) for Rows 2 and 4

¼ yd. Fabric D (blue sky print) for Row 4

⅛ yd. Fabric E (dark blue print) for Row 4

1 fat quarter Fabric F (city print) for Row 4

⅝ yd. Fabric G (light subtle print) for Rows 5 and 7

¼ yd. Fabric H (black and blue print) for Rows 5 and 7

¼ yd. Fabric I (black print) for Rows 9 and 11

¼ yd. Fabric J (yellow solid) for Rows 9 and 11

½ yd. fabric for binding

2 pieces, each 11" x 55" (minimum), of gridded lightweight fusible interfacing

2¼ yds. fabric for backing

40" x 78" piece of batting

*This is a ballpark figure, based on the specific theme print that I used. You may need to adjust this yardage, depending upon whether or not the strips or panels in your fabric run across the width of the fabric or parallel to the selvage. You'll also need to consider the width of the panels, the number of repeats, and so on.

Cutting and Piecing the Rows

Refer to "Quiltmaking Basics" on pages 6–16 for general construction techniques, and to the assembly diagram on page 34 for guidance as you piece each row.

All cutting measurements include ¼"-wide seam allowances.

Rows 1, 3, 6, 8, 10, and 12

From Fabric A, cut:

1 panel, 8" x 36½" for Row 1

1 panel, 7¾" x 36½" for Row 3

1 panel, 5¼" x 36½" for Row 6

1 panel, 8½" x 36½" for Row 8

1 panel, 8" x 36½" for Row 10

1 panel, 6½" x 36½" for Row 12

Row 2

Row Name: Stepping Stones

Finished Row Size: 36" x 4½"

¼ yd. *each* of Fabrics B and C

CUTTING

From Fabric B, cut:

1 strip, 2" x 42"

2 strips, each 2" x 18"

From Fabric C, cut:

2 strips, each 2" x 42"

1 strip, 2" x 18"

32

ASSEMBLY

1. With right sides together and long raw edges aligned, sew the 2" x 42" Fabric B strip between the two 2" x 42" Fabric C strips to make a 5" x 42" strip set. Press seams toward the B strip.

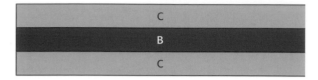

Make 1 strip set.

2. Crosscut the strip set into eight 3½" segments.

Cut 8.

3. Sew the 2" x 18" Fabric C strip between the two 2" x 18" Fabric B strips to make a 5" x 18" strip set. Press seams toward the B strips.

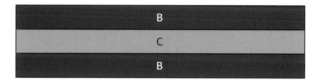

Make 1 strip set.

4. Crosscut the strip set into eight 2" segments.

Cut 8.

5. Join the units from steps 2 and 4, alternating them in a horizontal row. Begin the row with a step 2 segment. Press seams toward the step 2 segments.

Row 4

Block Name: Attic Window
Finished Block Size: 6"
⅛ yd. *each* of Fabrics C and E; 1 fat quarter Fabric F; ¼ yd. Fabric D

CUTTING

From *each* of Fabrics C and E, cut:

  5 rectangles, each 2" x 5"

  3 squares, each 2⅜" x 2⅜"; cut squares once diagonally to make 6 triangles. You'll have 1 extra triangle of each fabric; set these aside for another project.

From Fabric F, cut:

  5 squares, each 5" x 5"

From Fabric D, cut:

  2 strips, each 1½" x 36½"

  6 strips, each 1½" x 6½"

ASSEMBLY

1. With right sides together, sew a Fabric C and Fabric E triangle together along the long diagonal edge. Press seams toward the Fabric E triangle. Make 5.

2. Sew a unit from step 1 to the short edge of each 2" x 5" Fabric E rectangle, taking care to position the triangles as shown. Press seams toward the rectangle.

3. Sew a 2" x 5" Fabric C rectangle to the left side of each 5" Fabric F square. Press seams toward the rectangle.

4. Sew a unit from step 2 to the bottom edge of each unit from step 3. Press seams toward the bottom strip.

5. Sew a 1½" x 6½" Fabric D strip to the left side of each unit from step 4. Press seams toward the Fabric D strips.

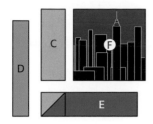

Make 5.

6. Join the 5 blocks in a horizontal row. Finish the row with the remaining 1½" x 6½" strip. Press seams to one side.

7. With right sides together, and matching centers and ends, pin and sew a 1½" x 36½" Fabric D strip to the top and bottom of the row.

Row 5

Row Name: Just a Big (City Girl!)

Finished Row Size: 36" x 7"

1 fat quarter Fabric H; ⅓ yd. Fabric G; 11" x 55" piece (minimum) of gridded lightweight fusible interfacing

CUTTING

From Fabric H, cut:

    81 squares, each 1½" x 1½"

From Fabric G, cut:

    178 squares, each 1½" x 1½"

ASSEMBLY

Refer to "Preprinted Fusible Interfacing" on page 11. The complete grid should measure 36 squares across by 7 squares down.

1. Using preprinted gridded fusible interfacing, lay the fusible interfacing, fusible side up, on a surface that can be ironed with a dry iron.

2. Refer to the diagram below, and beginning in the lower right-hand corner, place the 1½" Fabric D and E squares on the webbing to fill in the lettering and background. See the Alphabet/Number Chart on page 79 if you wish to use a different phrase in this row.

3. Follow the manufacturer's instructions to fuse the squares to the interfacing.

4. Sew the vertical and horizontal seam lines.

Row 7

Row Name: (Just a Big) City Girl!

Finished Row Size: 36" x 7"

1 fat quarter Fabric H; ⅓ yd. Fabric G; 11" x 55" piece (minimum) of gridded lightweight fusible interfacing

CUTTING

From Fabric H, cut:

    74 squares, each 1½" x 1½"

From Fabric G, cut:

    185 squares, each 1½" x 1½"

ASSEMBLY

Follow instructions for Row 5, steps 1–4 to create this row, using the 1½" Fabric G and Fabric H squares and placing the wording on the interfacing as shown below.

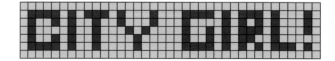

34

Rows 9 and 11

Row Name: Checkerboard
Finished Row Size: 36" x 3"
¼ yd. *each* of Fabrics I and J

CUTTING

From *each* of Fabrics I and J, cut:

3 strips, each 2" x 36"

ASSEMBLY

1. With right sides together and long raw edges aligned, sew a 2" x 36" Fabric I strip and a 2" x 36" Fabric J strip together to make a 3½" x 36" strip set. Press seams toward the Fabric I strip. Make 3 strip sets.

Make 3 strip sets.

2. Crosscut strip sets into a total of 48 segments, each 2" wide.

Cut 48.

3. Join 24 segments from step 2, taking care to position them as shown in the assembly diagram. Press seams to one side. Make 2 rows.

QUILT ASSEMBLY

Refer to the assembly diagram at right. Arrange Rows 1–12 as shown. With right sides together, and matching centers and ends, sew the rows together. Press seams in one direction.

> **Tip** This quilt does not include outside borders. It you wish, you may add them to enlarge the finished size of the quilt.

FINISHING

Refer to "Quilting" and "Finishing" on pages 13–16.

1. Center and layer the quilt top and the batting over the backing; baste.

2. Quilt as desired.

3. Trim the batting and backing even with the edges of the quilt top. Cut 6 strips, each 2 ½" x 42", from the binding fabric. Use these strips to make the binding; sew the binding to the quilt.

4. Make and attach a label to your quilt.

Kitties at Play

Terry Martin, 1999, Snohomish, Washington, 58½" x 79½";
machine quilted by Dizzy Stitches, hand quilted by Terry Martin.

▶ I HOPE YOU ENJOY MAKING THIS QUILT as much as I did. The nostalgic kitty prints are simply adorable and would look great in any bedroom that needs a feminine feline touch. But don't stop there! This quilt would work equally well in primary colors with airplane motifs for a masculine flavor, or in fall-colored leaf fabric for a rich autumn appeal. Use your imagination. Bar quilts are so versatile you could make this same quilt over and over again and never duplicate a look.

The attraction of specialty panels overwhelms me. I just can't resist them! If you don't have a specialty panel, you may eliminate it from the pieced block rows, remembering that this will shorten the overall length of the quilt. You could also choose one very lively print to substitute as a solid block, just to show off the fabric.

Materials (42"-wide fabric)

NOTE: Yardages listed are for the entire quilt as shown in the color photo on page 35. Instructions for each row indicate the yardage required for that row only.

8 squares, each 9½" x 9½", of conversation print panels or other theme fabric

1 fat quarter Fabric A (green print) for Row 1

¾ yd. Fabric B (yellow print) for middle border and Rows 1 and 3

½ yd. Fabric C (white floral print) for Rows 1 and 2

1 yd. Fabric D (pink print) for binding and Row 2

1⅝ yds. Fabric E (blue kitty print) for outside border and Row 3

1 yd. Fabric F (blue print) for sashing, inner border, and Row 4

⅜ yd. Fabric G (white solid) for Row 4

3¾ yds. fabric for backing

62" x 83" piece of batting

Cutting Sashing, Borders, and Binding

All cutting measurements include ¼"-wide seam allowances.

From Fabric F, cut:

10 strips, each 2½" x 42", for sashing and inner border

From Fabric B, cut:

6 strips, each 1½" x 42", for middle border

From Fabric E, cut:

7 strips, each 5½" x 42", for outer border

From Fabric D, cut:

7 strips, each 2½" x 42", for binding

Cutting and Piecing the Rows

Refer to "Quiltmaking Basics" on page 6 for general construction techniques and to the assembly diagram on page 39 for guidance as you piece each row.

All cutting measurements include ¼"-wide seam allowances.

Row 1

Block Name: Louisiana
Finished Block Size: 9"
1 fat quarter *each* of Fabrics A and B; ⅓ yd. Fabric C

CUTTING

From Fabric A, cut:

5 squares, each 5¾" x 5¾"; cut squares twice diagonally to make 20 triangles

From Fabric B, cut:

20 squares, each 3⅛" x 3⅛"; cut squares once diagonally to make 40 triangles

From Fabric C, cut:

20 rectangles, each 2¾" x 5"

ASSEMBLY

1. With right sides together, sew a Fabric B triangle to the short left side of each Fabric A triangle. Press seams toward the small triangle. Repeat to sew a Fabric B triangle to the short right side of the unit; press. Make 20.

2. Sew a 2¾" x 5" Fabric C rectangle to each unit from step 1 as shown. Press seams toward Fabric C. Make 20.

3. Sew units from step 2 in pairs, taking care to position them as shown. Press seams toward the Fabric A triangles. Make 10.

4. Sew units from step 3 in pairs as shown. Press seams in opposite directions from block to block. Make 5. Set the blocks aside for now.

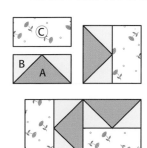
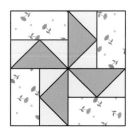

Make 5.

Row 2

Block Name: Spool and Bobbin
Finished Block Size: 9"
⅓ yd. *each* of Fabrics C and D

CUTTING

From Fabric C, cut:

5 squares, each 5⅜" x 5⅜"; cut squares once diagonally to make 10 triangles

10 squares, each 2¾" x 2¾"

From Fabric D, cut:

10 squares, each 5" x 5"

10 squares, each 3⅛" x 3⅛"; cut squares once diagonally to make 20 triangles

ASSEMBLY

1. With right sides together, sew a Fabric D triangle to 2 neighboring sides of each 2¾" Fabric C square. Press seams toward the triangles. Make 10.

2. Sew a unit from step 1 to a Fabric C triangle. Press seams away from the large triangles. Make 10.

3. Sew each unit from step 2 to a 5" Fabric D square. Press seams toward the squares. Make 10.

4. Sew units from step 3 in pairs as shown. Press seams in opposite directions from block to block. Make 5. Set the blocks aside for now.

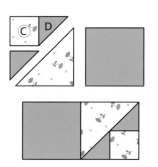
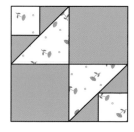

Make 5.

38

Row 3

Block Name: Sailboats
Finished Block Size: 9"
⅓ yd. Fabric B; ½ yd. Fabric E

CUTTING

From Fabric B, cut:

5 squares, each 5⅜" x 5⅜"; cut once diagonally to make 10 triangles

8 squares, each 4¼" x 4¼"; cut twice diagonally to make 32 triangles

From Fabric E, cut:

2 squares, each 10¼" x 10¼"; cut twice diagonally to make 8 triangles

5 squares, each 5⅜" x 5⅜"; cut once diagonally to make 10 triangles

4 squares, each 4¼" x 4¼"; cut twice diagonally to make 16 triangles

NOTE: You'll have a few triangles left over. Set them aside for another project.

ASSEMBLY

1. Join a small Fabric B and Fabric E triangle along the long diagonal edge. Press seams toward the Fabric E triangle. Make 15.

2. Sew a Fabric B triangle to the right edge of a unit from step 1, taking care to position the triangles as shown. Press seams toward the Fabric B triangle. Make 5.

3. Join 2 units from step 1 and a Fabric B triangle as shown. Press seams toward the step 1 units. Make 5.

4. Join a Fabric B triangle, a unit from step 2, and a unit from step 3 as shown. Press seams in one direction. Make 5.

5. Sew a large Fabric E triangle to each unit from step 4 as shown. Press seams toward the large triangle.

6. Turn each unit from step 5 on point. Sew 2 Fabric E triangles to the upper left and right sides of each step 5 unit. Press seams toward the Fabric E triangles. Repeat to sew a Fabric B triangle to the lower left and right sides of the unit; press. Make 5. Set the blocks aside for now.

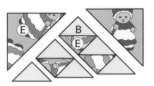

Make 5.

Row 4

Block Name: Shoo Fly
Finished Block Size: 9"
¼ yd. Fabric F; ⅜ yd. Fabric G

CUTTING

From Fabric F, cut:

10 squares, each 3⅞" x 3⅞"; cut squares once diagonally to make 20 triangles

5 squares, each 3½" x 3½"

From Fabric G, cut:

10 squares, each 3⅞" x 3⅞"; cut squares once diagonally to make 20 triangles

20 squares, each 3½" x 3½"

ASSEMBLY

1. Sew a 3½" Fabric F square between two 3½" Fabric G squares. Press seams toward the Fabric F square. Make 5.

2. Join a Fabric F and Fabric G triangle along the long diagonal edge. Press seams toward Fabric F. Make 20.

3. Sew a remaining 3½" Fabric G square between 2 units from step 2. Press seams away from the Fabric G square. Make 10.

4. Sew a unit from step 1 between 2 units from step 3. Press seams in opposite directions from block to block. Make 5.

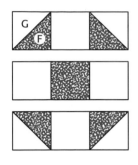
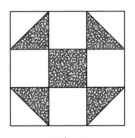

Make 5.

QUILT ASSEMBLY

Refer to the assembly diagram below and "Adding Borders" on page 12.

1. Arrange Rows 1–4, including two 9½" specialty blocks in each row as shown. Sew the blocks together to make 4 vertical rows. Press seams in one direction.

2. Sew the 2½" x 42" Fabric F strips together, end to end, to make a continuous 2½"-wide strip. From this strip, cut five 2½" x 63½" strips for the vertical sashing and side inner borders, and

two 2½" x 46½" strips for the top and bottom inner borders.

3. Place a 2½" x 63½" Fabric F strip between each vertical row. With right sides together, and matching center and ends, pin and sew the rows and sashing together. Press seams toward the sashing strips. Repeat to add a 2½" x 63½" sashing strip to the right and left sides of the quilt; press.

4. With rights sides together, and matching center and ends, pin and sew a 2½" x 46½" Fabric F strip to the top and bottom edges of the quilt. Press.

5. Sew the 1½" x 42" Fabric B middle border strips, end to end, to make a continuous 1½"-wide strip. Cut the border strips from this 1½"-wide strip; sew the strips first to the sides, then to the top and bottom.

6. Repeat step 5 to sew the outer borders to the quilt, using the 5½" x 42" Fabric E strips.

FINISHING

Refer to "Quilting" and "Finishing" on pages 13–16.

1. Divide the backing fabric crosswise into 2 equal panels of approximately 72" each. Remove the selvages and join the pieces to make a single large backing panel.

2. Position the backing so that the seam runs horizontally. Center and layer the quilt top and the batting over the backing; baste.

3. Quilt as desired.

4. Trim the batting and backing even with the edges of the quilt top. Use the 2½" x 42" Fabric D strips to make the binding; sew the binding to the quilt.

5. Make and attach a label to your quilt.

Paper-Doll Pink

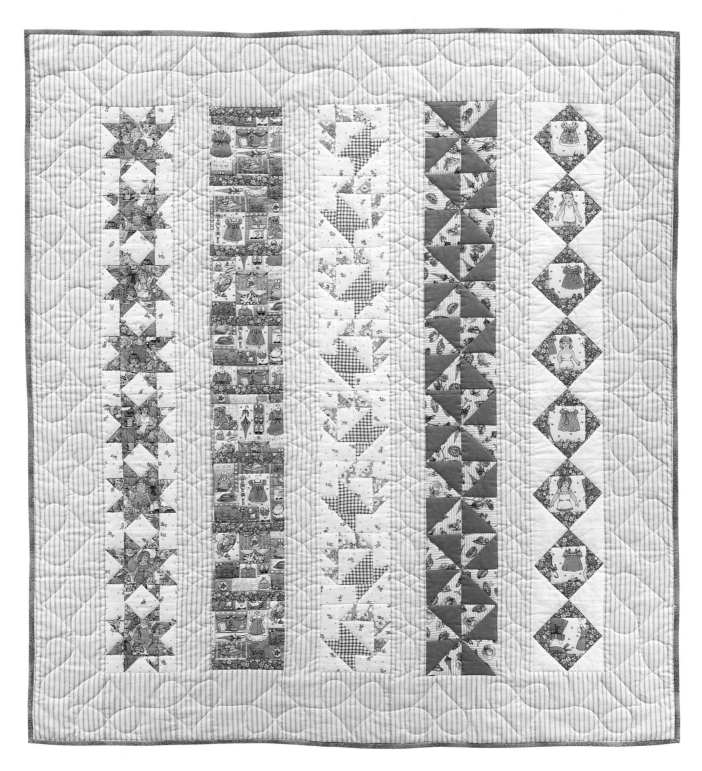

Terry Martin, 1999, Snohomish, Washington, 54½" x 60½";
machine quilted by Roxanne Carter, hand quilted by Terry Martin.

42

▶ WITH A SAD VOICE, I HAVE TO SAY that my daughter, McKenzie, was never a lover of dolls. She loves stuffed animals, and to this day selects fleece or fake fur so that I will make her a teddy bear. But no dolls! She has even given me the clothing from her American Girl doll (which resides in my bedroom) to dress a doll that was recently given to me.

When I was McKenzie's age, my great aunt subscribed to McCall's magazine, and she saved me the paper-doll page from every issue. For the life of me, I couldn't cut out the shapes! This quilt reminds me of those days gone by, especially with its pink ticking fabric.

A while back, I picked up a five-pack of fat quarters on sale at a local craft shop. It went into my "what do I do with these, but I must have them because they are so cute" drawer. It was with great joy that I rediscovered them for use in this bar quilt.

This quilt is very fat-quarter friendly. What a great way to use up small bits of fabric!

Materials (42"-wide fabric)

NOTE: Yardages listed are for the entire quilt as shown in the color photo on page 41. Instructions for each row indicate the yardage required for that row only.

1 fat quarter Fabric A (paper-doll print) for Row 1

⅔ yd. Fabric B (white floral print) for Rows 1 and 3

1 fat quarter Fabric C (multicolor print) for Row 2

1 fat quarter Fabric D (purple print) for Rows 2 and 5

⅛ yd. Fabric E (blue floral print) for Row 3

1 fat quarter Fabric F (pink check) for Row 3

1 fat quarter Fabric G (solid pink) for Row 4

1 fat quarter Fabric H (hat print) for Row 4

1 fat quarter Fabric I (dress print) for Row 5

1 fat quarter Fabric J (white print) for Row 5

1¾ yds. Fabric K (pink ticking) for sashing and border

½ yd. fabric for binding

3½ yds. fabric for backing

58" x 65" piece of batting

Cutting Sashing, Borders, and Binding

NOTE: Cut all Fabric K strips on the lengthwise grain (parallel to the selvage).

All cutting measurements include ¼"-wide seam allowances.

From Fabric K, cut:

    4 strips, each 3½" x 60½", for sashing

    2 strips, each 6½" x 60½", for side borders

    10 squares, each 6½" x 6½", for rows

From binding fabric, cut:

    6 strips, each 2½" x 42"

Cutting and Piecing the Rows

Refer to "Quiltmaking Basics" on page 6 for general construction techniques and to the assembly diagram on page 45 for guidance as you piece each row.

All cutting measurements include ¼"-wide seam allowances.

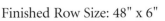

Row 1

Block Name: Sawtooth Star
Finished Block Size: 6"
1 fat quarter *each* of Fabrics A and B

CUTTING

From Fabric A, cut:

8 squares, each 3½" x 3½"

32 squares, each 2⅜" x 2⅜"; cut squares once diagonally to make 64 triangles

From Fabric B, cut:

8 squares, each 4¼" x 4¼"; cut squares twice diagonally to make 32 triangles

32 squares, each 2" x 2"

ASSEMBLY

1. Sew a Fabric A triangle to the short left side of each Fabric B triangle as shown. Press seams toward the small triangle. Repeat to sew a Fabric A triangle to the short right side of each unit as shown; press. Make 32.

2. Sew a 3½" Fabric A square between 2 units from step 1 as shown. Press seams away from the center square. Make 8.

3. Sew a remaining unit from step 1 between two 2" Fabric B squares as shown. Press seams away from the Fabric B squares. Make 16.

4. Sew a unit from step 2 between 2 units from step 3. Press seams in opposite directions from block to block. Make 8.

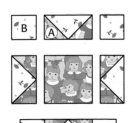 

Make 8.

5. Join the 8 blocks in a vertical row. Press seams in one direction.

Row 2

Finished Row Size: 48" x 6"
1 fat quarter *each* of Fabrics C and D

CUTTING

From Fabric C, cut:

8 rectangles, each 5½" x 6½"

From Fabric D, cut:

9 strips, each 1⅜" x 6½"

ASSEMBLY

Beginning with a 1⅜" x 6½" Fabric D strip, alternate the Fabric D strips with the 5½" x 6½" Fabric C rectangles to make a vertical row. Sew the strips and rectangles together; press seams toward the Fabric C rectangles.

Row 3

Block Name: Cake Stand
Finished Block Size: 6"
⅜ yd. Fabric B; ⅛ yd. Fabric E; 1 fat quarter Fabric F

CUTTING

From Fabric B, cut:

8 squares, each 3⅞" x 3⅞"; cut squares once diagonally to make 16 triangles

16 rectangles, each 2" x 3½"

16 squares, each 2⅜" x 2⅜"; cut squares once diagonally to make 32 triangles

8 squares, each 2" x 2"

From Fabric E, cut:

16 squares, each 2⅜" x 2⅜"; cut squares once diagonally to make 32 triangles

From Fabric F, cut:

4 squares, each 3⅞" x 3⅞"; cut squares once diagonally to make 8 triangles

8 squares, each 2⅜" x 2⅜"; cut squares once diagonally to make 16 triangles

44

ASSEMBLY

1. Sew a large Fabric B and Fabric F triangle together along the long diagonal edge. Press seams toward Fabric F. Make 8.

2. Repeat to sew a small Fabric B and Fabric E triangle together. Press seams toward Fabric E. Make 32.

3. Sew units from step 2 in pairs, taking care to position the triangles as shown. Press seams in one direction. Make 8 of each.

Make 8.   Make 8.

4. Sew a unit from step 3 to the left side of each unit from step 1. Press seams toward the center unit.

5. Join a 2" Fabric B square and a unit from step 3, taking care to position the triangles as shown. Press seams away from the Fabric B square. Make 8.

6. Sew a unit from step 5 to the top edge of each unit from step 4. Press seams toward the top unit.

7. Sew a small Fabric F triangle to a short end of a 2" x 3 ½" Fabric B rectangle as shown. Press seams toward the triangle. Make 8. Make 8 additional units, sewing the Fabric F triangle to the other end of a remaining 2" x 3 ½" Fabric B rectangle as shown; press.

Make 8.   Make 8.

8. Sew the first unit from step 7 (the one on the left) to the bottom edge of each unit from step 6 as shown. Press seams away from the step 6 unit. Repeat to sew the other unit from step 7 (the one on the right) to the right edge of the block as shown; press.

9. Sew a remaining large Fabric B triangle to the lower right corner of each unit from step 8. Press seams toward the Fabric B triangle.

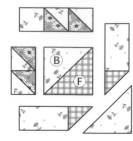 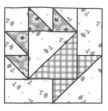

Make 8.

10. Join the 8 blocks in a vertical row, alternating the block's direction as shown in the assembly diagram. Press seams in one direction.

Row 4

Block Name: Pinwheel
Finished Block Size: 6"
1 fat quarter *each* of Fabrics G and H

CUTTING

From *each* of Fabrics G and H, cut:

16 squares, each 3⅞" x 3⅞"; cut squares once diagonally to make 32 triangles

ASSEMBLY

1. With right sides together and long diagonal edges aligned, sew a Fabric G and Fabric H triangle together. Press seams toward Fabric G. Make 32.

2. Sew units from step 1 in pairs, taking care to position them as shown. Press seams toward the Fabric G triangles. Make 16.

3. Sew units from step 2 in pairs as shown. Press seams in opposite directions from block to block. Make 8.

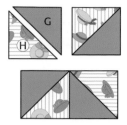

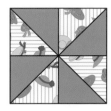

Make 8.

4. Join the 8 blocks in a vertical row. Press seams in one direction.

Row 5

Block Name: Economy Patch
Finished Block Size: 6"
1 fat quarter *each* of Fabrics D, J, and I

CUTTING

From Fabric D, cut:

8 squares, each 4¼" x 4¼"; cut squares twice diagonally to make 32 triangles

From Fabric J, cut:

16 squares, each 3⅞" x 3⅞"; cut squares once diagonally to make 32 triangles

From Fabric I, cut:

8 squares, each 3½" x 3½"

ASSEMBLY

1. Sew a Fabric D triangle to 2 opposite sides of each 3½" Fabric I square as shown. Press seams toward the triangles. Repeat to sew a Fabric D triangle to the remaining sides of the square. Press. Make 8.

2. Turn each unit from step 1 on point. Sew a Fabric J triangle to the upper left and lower right edges of each unit. Press seams toward the Fabric J triangles. Repeat to sew a Fabric J triangle to the lower left and upper right edges of each unit; press.

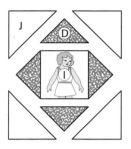

Make 8.

3. Join the 8 blocks in a vertical row. Press seams in one direction.

QUILT ASSEMBLY

Refer to the assembly diagram on page 46.

1. Sew a 6½" Fabric K square to the top and bottom edges of each vertical row. Press seams toward the Fabric K squares.

2. Arrange Rows 1–5, the four 3½" x 60½" Fabric K sashing strips, and the two 6½" x 60½" Fabric K border strips as shown. With right sides together, and matching centers and ends, pin and sew the rows, sashing, and borders together. Press the seams away from the pieced blocks.

FINISHING

Refer to "Quilting" and "Finishing" on pages 13–16.

1. Divide the backing fabric crosswise into 2 equal panels of approximately 63" each. Remove the selvages and join the pieces to make a single, large backing panel.

2. Position the backing so that the seam runs horizontally. Center and layer the quilt top and the batting over the backing; baste.

3. Quilt as desired.

4. Trim the batting and backing even with the edges of the quilt top. Use the 2½" x 42" strips to make the binding; sew the binding to the quilt.

5. Make and attach a label to your quilt.

Patriot's Pride

Terry Martin, 1999, Snohomish, Washington, 39½" x 50½".

48

▶ THIS IS A GREAT QUILT TO WHIP TOGETHER IN A WEEKEND. The blocks, such as Rail Fence and Flying Geese, are large and simple. Although I included an appliquéd block—the only one in the book!—you'll find that when you use a simple machine stitch to secure the appliqué, it all goes together quickly.

I had just one fat quarter of the very large print I used for the heart, so I pulled out my heart cookie cutter from Valentine's Day and centered it over the motifs I wanted to emphasize. It worked! The monochromatic background toned down the wild print, and the golden eagles, framed inside the heart, are majestic.

I have a secret (and this is exactly the reason I love conversation/specialty fabric). The pinwheels in Row 2 are not pieced blocks! They are cut from one piece of fabric. I fussy-cut the fabric so that when the vertical seams were stitched, the pinwheel "block" was left. This is a real advantage to bar quilts; if you have a preprinted fabric like the pinwheel, you can fussy-cut and include it. Width doesn't matter, as long as the strip is the correct length, and even that can be fudged!

Machine quilting this quilt was fun as I attempted to add a folk art flair with very primitive quilting. Although I slightly terrified the editorial staff at Martingale & Company when I announced that my first attempt at machine quilting would be for this book, I was pleased with the results. They're breathing easier now, too.

Materials (42"-wide fabric)

NOTE: Yardages listed are for the entire quilt. Instructions for each row indicate the yardage required for that row only.

¼ yd. Fabric A (navy blue flag print) for Row 1

¼ yd. Fabric B (red, white, and blue flag print) for Row 1

¾ yd. Fabric C (light star print) for Rows 1, 3, 4, and 5

¼ yd. Fabric D (dark blue solid) for sashing

⅓ yd. Fabric E (pinwheel "panel" print) for Row 2*

1 fat quarter Fabric F (navy blue star print) for Rows 3 and 5

⅓ yd. Fabric G (red star print) for Row 3

⅔ yd. Fabric H (large-scale red-white-and-blue print) for sashing and binding

1 fat quarter Fabric I (eagle print) for Row 4

1 fat quarter *each* Fabric J, K, and L (different blue prints) for Row 5

1 fat quarter Fabric M (gold print) for Row 5

¼ yd. Fabric N (red solid) for border

1⅝ yds. fabric for backing

43" x 54" piece of batting

* This is a "ballpark" figure, based on the specific fabric that I used. You may need to adjust this yardage (and/or piece the strip), depending upon whether the motif in your fabric runs across the width of the fabric or parallel to the selvage.

Cutting Sashing, Borders, and Binding

All cutting measurements include ¼"-wide seam allowances.

From Fabric D, cut:

3 strips, each 1½" x 42", for sashing

From Fabric H, cut:

3 strips, each 2" x 42", for sashing

5 strips, each 2½" x 42", for binding

From Fabric N, cut:

5 strips, each 1½" x 42", for border

Cutting and Piecing the Rows

Refer to "Quiltmaking Basics" on page 6 for general construction techniques and to the assembly diagram on page 52 for guidance as you piece each row.

All cutting measurements include ¼"-wide seam allowances.

Row 1

Block Name: Rail Fence
Finished Block Size: 6"
¼ yd. *each* Fabrics A, B, and C

CUTTING

From *each* of Fabrics A, B, and C, cut:

2 strips, each 2½" x 42"

ASSEMBLY

1. With right sides together and long raw edges aligned, sew one 2½" x 42" strip each of Fabrics A, B, and C together in that order to make a 6½" x 42" strip set. Press seams in one direction. Make 2 strip sets.

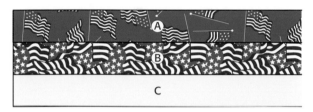

Make 2 strip sets.

2. Crosscut the strip sets into a total of eight 6½" segments.

Cut 8.

3. Join the 8 segments, taking care to position them as shown in the assembly diagram. Press seams in one direction.

Row 2

Row Name: Faux Pinwheel
Finished Row Size: 4" x 48"
⅓ yd. Fabric E*

*See note on page 48.

From Fabric E, cut:

1 strip or panel, 4½" x 48½"

You can adjust the width of this row to fit the "block" motif of the specialty print you have chosen. If necessary, add spacer pieces to the top and bottom of the strip so that the row finishes to the correct vertical measurement; in this case, 48".

Row 3

Block Name: USA Flag
Finished Block Size: 10" x 8"
1 fat quarter Fabric F; ⅓ yd. *each* of Fabrics C and G

CUTTING

From Fabric F, cut:

6 squares, each 4½" x 4½"

From *each* of Fabrics C and G, cut:

6 strips, each 1½" x 42"

ASSEMBLY

1. With right sides together and long raw edges aligned, sew 1½" x 42" Fabric C and G strips together in the following order to make a 4½" x 42" strip set: Fabric G, Fabric C, Fabric G, and Fabric C. Press seams toward the Fabric G strips. Make 3 strip sets.

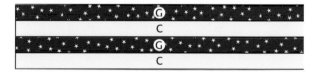

Make 3 strip sets.

2. Crosscut 1 strip set into six 6½" segments. From the remaining strip sets, cut a total of six 10½" segments.

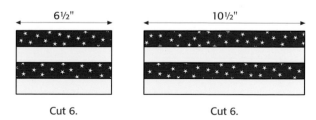

Cut 6.   Cut 6.

50

3. Sew a 4½" Fabric F square to the short left edge of each 6½" segment from step 2, taking care to position the strips as shown. Press seams toward the squares. Make 6.

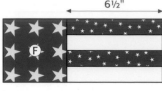

6½"

Make 6.

4. Sew a 10½" segment from step 2 to the bottom edge of each unit from step 3, taking care to position the strips as shown. Press seams toward the bottom segment.

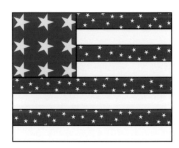

Make 6.

5. Join the 6 blocks in a vertical row. Press seams in one direction.

Row 4

Block Name: Heart Appliqué
Finished Block Size: 6"
¼ yd. Fabric C; 1 fat quarter Fabric I

CUTTING

From Fabric C, cut:

8 squares, each 6½" x 6½"

ASSEMBLY

The appliqué in this block is completed using a machine blanket stitch. The hearts are cut to finished size with no seam allowance added. If you prefer, you may use a more traditional appliqué method to stitch the hearts in place.

1. Use the heart pattern on page 52 to make a template. Trace the template and cut 8 hearts from Fabric I.

2. Center a heart appliqué on each 6½" Fabric C square; press and pin in place.

> **Tip** If you'd like, use a fusible web to bond the appliqué hearts to the background squares. Follow the manufacturer's instructions to apply the fusible web.

3. Machine stitch the heart to the background square with a small blanket stitch. Or, if you prefer, work the blanket stitch by hand in a contrasting thread.

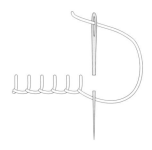

4. Join the 8 blocks in a vertical row. Press seams in one direction.

Row 5

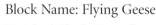

Block Name: Flying Geese
Finished Block Size: 6"
1 fat quarter *each* of Fabrics F, J, K, and L; ⅛ yd. *each* of Fabrics C and M

CUTTING

From *each* of Fabrics F, J, K, and L, cut:

1 square, 7⅛" x 7⅛"; cut square twice diagonally to make 4 triangles

From *each* of Fabrics C and M, cut:

8 squares, each 3⅞" x 3⅞"; cut squares once diagonally to make 16 triangles

ASSEMBLY

1. With right sides together, sew a Fabric C or M triangle to the short left side of a Fabric F, J, K, or L triangle. Press seams toward the small triangle. Repeat to sew a matching small triangle to the short right side of the unit as shown; press. Make 16 units, randomly pairing large and small triangle fabrics.

Make 16.

2. Sew units from step 1 in random pairs. Press seams toward the top unit. Make 8.

Make 8.

3. Join the 8 blocks in a vertical row. Press seams toward the top of the row.

QUILT ASSEMBLY

Refer to the assembly diagram on page 52.

1. Sew the 1½" x 42" Fabric D sashing strips together, end to end, to make a continuous 1½"-wide strip. Cut two 1½" x 48½" sashing strips from this pieced strip.

2. With right sides together, and matching centers and ends, pin and sew a trimmed sashing strip to the left and right sides of Row 2. Press seams toward the sashing strips.

3. Repeat steps 1 and 2 to add sashing to the left and right sides of Row 4, using the 2" x 42" Fabric H strips.

4. Arrange Rows 1–5 as shown in the assembly diagram. With right sides together, and matching centers and ends, pin and sew the rows together. Press seams toward the sashing strips.

ADDING THE BORDERS

Refer to "Adding the Borders" on page 12.

Sew the 1½" x 42" Fabric N border strips together, end to end, to make a continuous 1½"-wide strip. Cut the border strips from this 1½"-wide strip; sew the strips first to the sides, then to the top and bottom.

FINISHING

Refer to "Quilting" and "Finishing" on pages 13–16.

1. Center and layer the quilt top and the batting over the backing; baste.

2. Quilt as desired.

3. Trim the batting and backing even with the edges of the quilt top. Use the 2½" x 42" Fabric H strips to make the binding; sew the binding to the quilt.

4. Make and attach a label to your quilt.

Heart
Cut 8

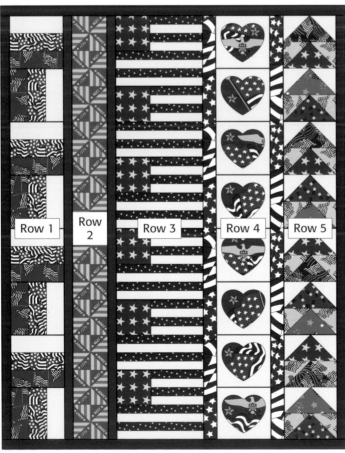

Row 1

Row 2

Row 3

Row 4

Row 5

Rugrats Rule, Adults Drool

Terry Martin, 1999, Snohomish, Washington, 65½" x 67½"; machine quilted by Sue Lohse.

54

▶ MY HUSBAND, ED, FIRST SPIED THE RUGRATS fabric at our local fabric store. To my dismay, it was a single fat quarter, and that's all there was. I knew I'd need more to use as the focal fabric in a quilt. The search was on, and within a week I held five precious yards in my hand. In the meantime, Ed, in the true spirit of an understanding quilter's husband, found several fat quarters to complement the Rugrats fabric. Thus "Rugrats Rule, Adults Drool" was born.

Two frequent visitors to our house are Madeleine, age 8, and Daniel, age 5. Both have given this quilt a hearty thumbs-up. But don't limit this quilt to a kid's print. These are great blocks to use with any theme fabric.

Materials (42"-wide fabric)

NOTE: Yardages listed are for the entire quilt as shown in the color photo on page 53. Instructions for each row indicate the yardage for that row only.

1 fat quarter Fabric A (number print) for Rows 1 and 3

1 fat quarter Fabric B (red bubble print) for Rows 1 and 3

⅝ yd. Fabric C (yellow solid) for inner border and Rows 1 and 3

⅓ yd. Fabric D (blue star print) for Rows 2 and 3

¼ yd. Fabric E (white bubble print) for Rows 2 and 3

1 fat quarter Fabric F (rainbow stripe) for Rows 3 and 5

½ yd. Fabric G (heart print) for Rows 3 and 4

1 fat quarter Fabric H (orange print) for Rows 3 and 5

1½ yds. Fabric I (Rugrats print) for outer border and Row 3

½ yd. Fabric J (orange solid) for sashing and Row 3

1 fat quarter Fabric K (teal print) for Row 4

⅝ yd. fabric for binding

4 yds. fabric for backing

70" x 71" piece of batting

Cutting the Sashing, Borders, and Binding

All measurements include ¼"-wide seam allowances.

From Fabric J, cut:

5 strips, each 2½" x 42, for sashing

From Fabric C, cut:

5 strips, each 2½" x 42", for inner border

From Fabric I, cut:

6 strips, each 8½" x 42", for outer border

From binding fabric, cut:

7 strips, each 2½" x 42"

Cutting and Piecing the Rows

Refer to "Quiltmaking Basics" on page 6 for general construction techniques, and to the quilt assembly diagram on page 58 for guidance as you piece each row.

All cutting measurements include ¼"-wide seam allowances.

Row 1

Block Name: Birds in the Air

Finished Block Size: 9"

1 fat quarter *each* Fabrics A, B, and C

CUTTING

From Fabric A, cut:

5 squares, each 6½" x 6½"

From *each* of Fabrics B and C, cut:

13 squares, each 3⅞" x 3⅞"; cut squares once diagonally to make 26 triangles

NOTE: You'll have one triangle of Fabric B and one of Fabric C left over. Set them aside for another project.

ASSEMBLY

1. Sew a Fabric B and Fabric C triangle together along the long diagonal edge. Press seams toward Fabric B. Make 25.
2. Sew 2 units from step 1 together, taking care to position the triangles as shown. Press seams to one side. Make 5.
3. Sew a unit from step 2 to the top edge of each 6½" Fabric A square. Press seams toward the Fabric A square.
4. Sew 3 units from step 1 together, taking care to position the triangles as shown. Press seams to one side. Make 5.
5. Sew a unit from step 4 to the right edge of each unit from step 3 as shown. Press seams away from the step 3 units.

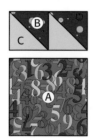  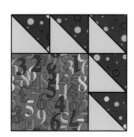

Make 5.

6. Join the 5 blocks in a horizontal row as shown in the assembly diagram. Press seams to one side.

Row 2

Block Name: Four Patch

Finished Block Size: 5"

⅓ yd. Fabric D; ⅛ yd. Fabric E

CUTTING

From Fabric D, cut:

18 squares, each 3" x 3"

2 strips, each 1¾" x 42"

From Fabric E, cut:

2 strips, each 1¾" x 42"

ASSEMBLY

1. With right sides together and long raw edges aligned, sew a 1¾" x 42" Fabric D and 1¾" x 42" Fabric E strip together to make a 3" x 42" strip set. Press seams toward the Fabric D strip. Make 2 strip sets.

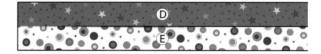

Make 2 strip sets.

2. Crosscut the strip sets into a total of 36 segments, each 1¾" wide.

Cut 36 segments.

3. Sew units from step 2 in pairs as shown on page 56. Press seams to one side. Make 18.
4. Sew a unit from step 3 to each 3" Fabric D square, taking care to position the four-patch unit as shown. Press seams toward the Fabric D square. Make 18.

56

5. Sew units from step 4 in pairs, taking care to position the four-patch units as shown. Press seams to one side. Make 9.

Make 9.

6. Join the 9 blocks in a horizontal row, alternating the blocks' direction as shown. Press seams to one side.

Row 3

Block Name: Log Cabin
Finished Block Size: 10"
Scraps of Fabrics A–J

CUTTING

From Fabric I, cut:
    4 squares, each 4½" x 4½"
From Fabric H, cut:
    4 strips, each 2" x 4½"
From *each* of Fabrics G and B, cut:
    4 strips, each 2" x 6"
From *each* of Fabrics F and C, cut:
    4 strips, each 2" x 7½"
From *each* of Fabrics A and E, cut:
    4 strips, each 2" x 9"
From Fabric D, cut:
    4 strips, each 2" x 10½"
From Fabric J, cut:
    3 strips, each 2¼" x 10½"

ASSEMBLY

1. With right sides together, sew a 2" x 4½" Fabric H strip to the bottom edge of each 4½" Fabric I square. Press seams away from the square. Make 4.

2. Working counterclockwise, sew strips to each unit from step 1 in the following order: 1 each of Fabric G, B, F, C, A, E, and D. As each strip is added, press seams away from the Fabric I square.

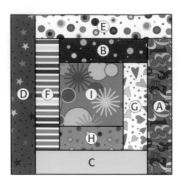

3. Join the 4 blocks in a horizontal row, separating each block with a 2¼" x 10½" Fabric J strip. Press seams toward the Fabric J strips.

Row 4

Block Name: Free Trade
Finished Block Size: 9"
½ yd. Fabric G; 1 fat quarter Fabric K

CUTTING

From Fabric G, cut:
    5 squares, each 5¾" x 5¾"; cut squares twice diagonally to make 20 triangles
    5 squares, each 3⅛" x 3⅛"; cut squares once diagonally to make 10 triangles
    30 squares, each 2¾" x 2¾"
From Fabric K, cut:
    25 squares, each 3⅛" x 3⅛"; cut squares once diagonally to make 50 triangles.

ASSEMBLY

1. Sew a small Fabric G and Fabric K triangle together along the long diagonal edge. Press seams toward Fabric K. Make 10.

2. Sew a 2¾" Fabric G square to each unit from step 1, taking care to position the triangles as shown. Press seams toward the squares.

3. Sew units from step 2 in pairs as shown. Press seams to one side. Make 5.

4. With right sides together, sew a remaining Fabric K triangle to the short left side of each large Fabric G triangle as shown. Press seams toward the small triangle. Repeat to sew a Fabric K triangle to the short right side of the unit as shown; press. Make 20.

5. Sew each unit from step 3 between 2 units from step 4 as shown. Press seams away from the center unit.

6. Sew each remaining unit from step 4 between two 2¾" Fabric G squares. Press seams away from the Fabric G squares. Make 10.

7. Sew each unit from step 5 between two units from step 6 as shown. Press seams in opposite directions from block to block.

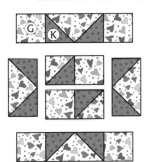 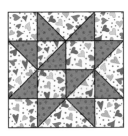

Make 5.

8. Join the 5 blocks in a horizontal row. Press seams to one side.

Row 5

Block Name: Pinwheel

Block Size: 6"

1 fat quarter *each* of Fabrics F and H

CUTTING

From *each* of Fabrics F and H, cut:

15 squares, each 3⅞" x 3⅞"; cut squares once diagonally to make 30 triangles

ASSEMBLY

1. Sew a Fabric F and Fabric H triangle together along the long diagonal edge. Press seams toward Fabric H. Make 30.

2. Sew units from step 1 in pairs, taking care to position them as shown. Press seams toward the H triangles. Make 15.

3. Sew units from step 2 in pairs as shown. Press seams in opposite directions from block to block. Make 7 blocks. You'll have one ½-block unit left over.

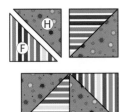 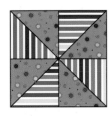

Make 7.

4. Join the 7 blocks in a horizontal row, with the ½-block unit at the start of the row. Press seams to one side.

QUILT ASSEMBLY

Refer to the assembly diagram on page 58.

1. Sew the 2½" x 42" Fabric J sashing strips together, end to end, to make a continuous 2½"-wide strip. Cut four 2½" x 45½" sashing strips from this pieced strip.

2. Arrange Rows 1–5 and the four 2½" x 45½" sashing strips as shown. With right sides together, and matching centers and ends, pin and sew the rows and sashing strips together. Press seams toward the sashing strips.

58

ADDING THE BORDERS

Refer to "Adding the Borders" on page 12.

1. Sew the 2½" x 42" Fabric C inner border strips together, end to end, to make a continuous 2½"-wide strip. Cut the border strips from the 2½"-wide strip; sew the strips first to the sides, then to the top and bottom.

2. Repeat step 1 to sew the outer borders to the quilt, using the 8½" x 42" Fabric I strips.

FINISHING

Refer to "Quilting" and "Finishing" on pages 13–16.

1. Divide the backing fabric crosswise into 2 equal panels of approximately 72" each. Remove the selvages and join the pieces to make a single, large backing panel.

2. Center and layer the quilt top and the batting over the backing; baste.

3. Quilt as desired.

4. Trim the batting and backing even with the edges of the quilt top. Use the 2½" x 42" strips to make the binding; sew the binding to the quilt.

5. Make and attach a label to your quilt.

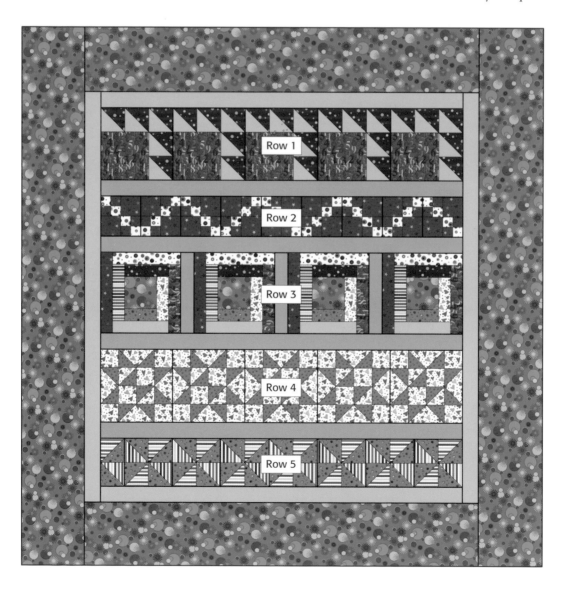

Silver and Ice

Terry Martin, 1999, Snohomish, Washington, 55½" x 30"; machine quilted by Dizzy Stitches.

▶ INSPIRATION FOR A QUILT DESIGN CAN COME from a variety of different sources: postcard art, stationery, fabric, friends, family, and co-workers, to name just a few. It is a good notion to pay attention to all of them and to let your imagination run free.

My co-worker Beth Kovich, who wanted a quilt that would fit over a mantelpiece, inspired this quilt. What great fun! I instantly envisioned the nontraditional size—something wide, but not too tall.

Next came the fabric. I love blue and silver! The new glitter fabrics were perfect. Can't you just imagine this quilt atop a mantel, with candles picking up the fabric's sparkle?

To me, this icy blue color scheme suggests the dead of winter. But the simple star, tree, and house design would look great in the colors of all the seasons: rusts, golds, and browns for fall; pastel yellows, pinks, and periwinkles for spring; and brilliant, rich greens, oranges, reds, and purples for summer. Since the mantel is often the focal point of a room, changing this quilt with the season is a fast and easy way to freshen the decor. Add coordinating mantel accessories, as well as throw pillows or quilts in the appropriate colors, and your home is ready for the changing seasons. You won't break your pocketbook—or need to pull out the interior-design manuals!

Materials (42"-wide fabric)

NOTE: Yardages listed are for the entire quilt as shown in the color photo on page 59. Instructions for each row indicate the yardage required for that row only.

⅔ yd. Fabric A (white tone-on-tone print) for corners and Rows 1, 2, 3, and 4

½ yd. Fabric B (dark blue and white star print) for Rows 1 and 3

⅓ yd. Fabric C (dark blue and silver star print) for sashing, corners, and Rows 2 and 3

⅞ yd. Fabric D (blue and purple packages print) for outer border, corners, and Rows 2 and 3

⅛ yd. Fabric E (navy blue and white print) for corners and Rows 2 and 3

⅓ yd. Fabric F (light blue print) for corners and Rows 2, 3, and 4

⅛ yd. Fabric G (dark blue snowflake print) for Row 2

⅝ yd. Fabric H (purple tone-on-tone print) for inner border, binding, and Row 3

1⅔ yds. fabric for backing

59" x 34" piece of batting

Cutting Sashing, Borders, and Binding

All measurements include ¼"-wide seam allowances.

From Fabric C, cut:

1 strip, 1½" x 44½" for sashing; this strip will need to be pieced

From Fabric H, cut:

3 strips, each 1½" x 42", for top and bottom inner border

2 strips, each 1½" x 18¾", for side inner border

5 strips, each 2½" x 42", for binding

From Fabric D, cut:

3 strips, each 5¼" x 42", for top and bottom outer border

2 strips, each 5" x 18¾", for side outer border

Cutting and Piecing the Rows

Refer to "Quiltmaking Basics" on page 6 for general construction techniques and to the assembly diagram on page 64 for guidance as you piece each row.

All cutting measurements include ¼"-wide seam allowances.

Row 1

Block Name: Turnstile
Finished Block Size: 4"
1 fat quarter Fabric A; ⅓ yd. Fabric B

CUTTING

From Fabric A, cut:

11 squares, each 3¼" x 3¼"; cut squares twice diagonally to make 44 triangles

From Fabric B, cut:

11 squares, each 3¼" x 3¼"; cut squares twice diagonally to make 44 triangles

22 squares, each 2⅞" x 2⅞"; cut squares once diagonally to make 44 triangles

ASSEMBLY

1. Sew a small Fabric A triangle and Fabric B triangle together on one short side. Press seams toward Fabric B. Make 44.

2. Sew a large Fabric B triangle to each unit from step 1 as shown. Press the seams toward the step 1 unit.

3. Sew units from step 2 in pairs, taking care to position them as shown. Press seams toward the Fabric A triangles. Make 22.

4. Sew units from step 3 in pairs as shown. Press seams in opposite directions from block to block. Make 11.

Make 11.

5. Join the 11 blocks in a horizontal row. Press seams to one side.

Row 2

Block Name: Tree

Finished Block Size: 5½" x 5¾"

⅛ yard *each* of Fabrics C, D, E, F, and G; ¼ yd. Fabric A; scrap of Fabric D

CUTTING

From *each* of Fabrics C, D, E, F, and G, cut:

 1 strip, 1½" x 42"

From Fabric A, cut:

 12 rectangles, each 3½" x 5⅞"

 2 strips, each 2½" x 20"

From Fabric D, cut:

 1 strip, 2" x 20"

ASSEMBLY

1. Arrange the 1½" x 42" Fabric C, D, E, F, and G strips in any visually pleasing, random order. With right sides together and long raw edges aligned, sew the strips together to make a 5½" x 42" strip set. Press seams to one side.

2. Carefully align the 60-degree marking of your long acrylic ruler with the top edge of the strip set. Use your rotary cutter to make the resulting diagonal cut through the strip set.

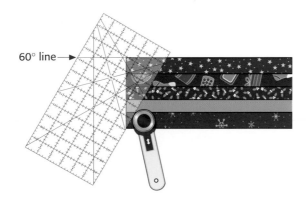

60° line →

3. Flip the ruler, aligning the 60-degree marking with the strip set's top edge so that the bottom edge of the resulting triangle measures 6⅜". Use your rotary cutter to make this mirror-image diagonal cut.

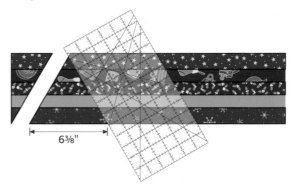

6⅜"

4. Continue flipping the ruler and cutting until you have cut 12 triangular tree units. Be sure to retrim as necessary so you are always beginning with a "clean" 60-degree cut.

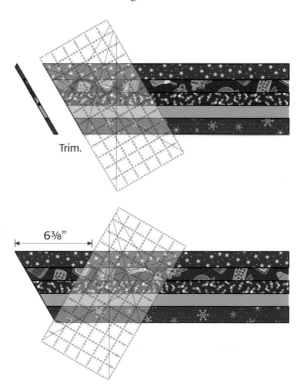

Trim.

6⅜"

62

5. Cut six 3½" x 5⅞" Fabric A rectangles once diagonally in one direction to make 12 skinny triangles. Cut the remaining six 3½" x 5⅞" Fabric A rectangles diagonally in the other direction as shown to make the opposite 12 skinny triangles.

Cut 6.   Cut 6.

6. Sew a Fabric A triangle to the left side of each tree unit as shown. Press seams toward the Fabric A triangles. Repeat to sew a Fabric A triangle to the right side of each unit; press.

Make 12.

7. Sew the 2" x 20" Fabric D strip between the 2½" x 20" Fabric A strips to make a 6" x 20" strip set. Press seams toward Fabric D.

Make 1 strip set.

8. Crosscut the strip set into twelve 1½" segments.

1½"

Cut 12.

9. Sew a segment from step 8 to the bottom edge of each unit from step 6. Press seams toward the bottom edge of the block. Make 12.

10. Join 8 blocks in a horizontal row. Press seams to one side. Set the remaining 4 blocks aside for the corner blocks of the quilt.

Row 3

Block Name: House

Finished Block Size: 4" x 5½"

1 fat quarter *each* of Fabrics A, B, C, D, and F; scraps of Fabrics E and H

CUTTING

From Fabric A, cut:

    11 squares, each 2⅞" x 2⅞" (roof unit); cut once diagonally to make 22 triangles

    3 rectangles, each 1½" x 3" (doors)

    3 rectangles, each 1½" x 1¾" (windows)

From *each* of Fabrics B and D, cut:

    1 square, 5¼" x 5¼" (roofs)*

    3 rectangles, each 1½" x 4½" (houses)

    6 rectangles, each 1¼" x 3" (houses)

    3 rectangles, each 1½" x 1¾" (houses)

    3 rectangles, each 1" x 3" (houses)

From Fabric C, cut:

    1 square, 5¼" x 5¼" (roofs)*

    2 rectangles, each 1½" x 4½" (houses)

    4 rectangles, each 1¼" x 3" (houses)

    2 rectangles, each 1½" x 1¾" (houses)

    2 rectangles, each 1" x 3" (houses)

From Fabric F, cut:

    1 square, 5¼" x 5¼" (roofs)*

    3 rectangles, each 1½" x 4½" (houses)

    6 rectangles, each 1¼" x 3" (houses)

    5 rectangles, each 1½" x 1¾" (houses and windows)

    3 rectangles, each 1" x 3" (houses)

    2 rectangles, each 1½" x 3" (doors)

From *each* of Fabric E and H, cut:

    3 rectangles, each 1½" x 3" (doors)

    3 rectangles, each 1½" x 1¾" (windows)

* Cut each 5¼" Fabric B, D, C, and F square twice diagonally to make 4 triangles. You will need 11 of these triangles: 3 triangles each of Fabric B, D, and F, and 2 of Fabric C. Set the rest aside for another project.

ASSEMBLY

You will be making 11 house blocks. For each block, piece the house from one fabric (either B, D, C, or F), and the door and window from another (either A, E, F, or H).

1. Sew a Fabric A triangle to the short left side of each of the 11 Fabric B, D, C, and F triangles. Press seams toward Fabric A. Repeat to sew a Fabric A triangle to the short right side of each unit as shown; press.

2. Sew a matching-color Fabric B, D, C, or F (house) 1½" x 4½" rectangle to the bottom edge of each roof unit from step 1. Press seams toward the rectangles.

3. Sew a 1½" x 1¾" Fabric B, D, C, or F (house) rectangle to a 1½" x 1¾" Fabric A, E, F, or H (window) rectangle. Press seams away from the window rectangle. Make 11.

4. Sew a matching-color 1" x 3" Fabric B, D, C, or F (house) rectangle to the right edge of each unit from step 3. Press the seams toward the new strip.

5. Using the same fabric combinations that you used in step 3, sew a 1½" x 3" Fabric A, E, F, or H (door) rectangle between two 1¼" x 3" Fabric B, D, C, or F (house) rectangles. Press seams away from the "door." Make 11.

6. Sew a unit from step 5 to the left edge of a matching-color unit from step 4. Press seams to one side.

7. Sew a unit from step 2 to the top edge of a matching-color unit from step 6. Press seams toward the top unit.

Make 11.

8. Join the 11 blocks in a horizontal row. Press seams to one side.

Row 4

Row Name: Checkered Sidewalk

Finished Row Size: 44" x 2"

⅛ yd. *each* of Fabrics A and F

CUTTING

From *each* of Fabrics A and F, cut:

2 strips, each 1½" x 42"

ASSEMBLY

1. With right sides together and long raw edges aligned, sew a 1½" x 42" Fabric A strip to a 1½" x 42" Fabric F strip to make a 2½" x 42" strip set. Press seams toward Fabric F. Make 2 strip sets.

Make 2 strip sets.

2. Crosscut the strip sets into a total of 22 segments, each 2½" wide.

Cut 22.

3. Join the 22 segments from step 2, taking care to position them as shown in the assembly diagram. Press seams to one side.

QUILT ASSEMBLY

Refer to the assembly diagram on page 64. Arrange Rows 1–4, positioning the 1½" x 44½" Fabric C sashing strip between rows 2 and 3. With right sides together, and matching centers and ends, pin and sew the rows and sashing together. Press seams toward the sashing strip in the center of the quilt.

ADDING THE BORDERS

Refer to "Adding Borders" on page 12.

1. Sew the three 1½" x 42" Fabric H top and bottom inner border strips, end to end, to make a continuous 1½"-wide strip. Repeat with the 5¼" x 42" Fabric D top and bottom outer border strips.

2. With right sides together and long raw edges aligned, sew the pieced Fabric H and Fabric D top and bottom border strips together to make a 6¼"-wide strip set. Press seams toward Fabric D. From this strip set, cut two 6¼" x 44½" border units.

3. With right sides together, and matching centers and ends, pin the border units from step 2 to the top and bottom edges of the quilt. Be sure the narrow Fabric H strip is closest to the center of the quilt. Sew, and then press seams toward the border units.

4. With right sides together and long raw edges aligned, sew a 1½" x 18¾" Fabric H side inner border strip to each 5" x 18¾" Fabric D side outer border strip to make 2 border units. Press seams toward Fabric D.

5. Sew a remaining Tree block to the short ends of each side border unit, taking care to position the blocks as shown below. Press seams toward the border units.

6. Refer to the color photo on page 59. With right sides together, and matching key points, pin and sew the appropriate side border unit to each side of the quilt; press.

FINISHING

Refer to "Quilting" and "Finishing" on pages 13–16.

1. Center and layer the quilt top and the batting over the backing; baste.

2. Quilt as desired.

3. Trim the batting and backing even with the edges of the quilt top. Use the 2½" x 42" Fabric H strips to make the binding; sew the binding to the quilt.

4. Make and attach a label to your quilt.

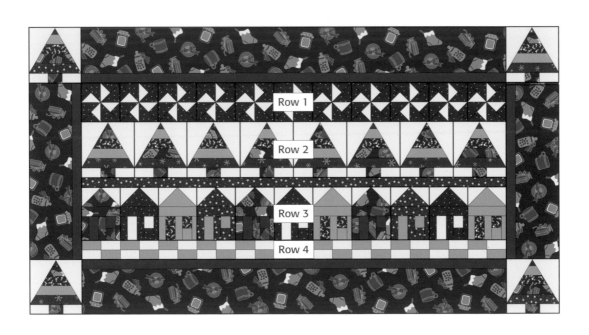

Terry Martin, 1999, Snohomish, Washington, 62½" x 95½"; machine quilted by Sue Lohse.

▶ THE CONCEPT FOR THIS QUILT CAME TO ME as I was heading to a quilt shop with my best friend, Cornelia. Sometimes I do my best thinking and design work in the car or the shower. If this happens to you too, write those thoughts down as soon as possible. You will be amazed at the great ideas that pop up—and you can have a good laugh later at the silly ones.

Assembling the stylized Christmas tree is fun and fast, since there are few blocks. Yet it makes up into a rather large quilt that you can use on a bed or display on a spacious wall. Because of its size, I chose not to include any borders, but I did add a contrasting 1"-wide binding to create a simple "frame."

I treated myself to some luscious Hoffman fabrics for this quilt, and I had a lot of fun thinking of the elements of a Christmas tree while choosing the blocks. The Right Hand of Friendship block makes the perfect choice for the star atop the tree, and Contrary Wife and Old Maid's Puzzle add movement, like draped garland, to the design. I incorporated two different pine cone prints for the tree trunk to give it added texture.

Materials (42"-wide fabrics)

NOTE: Yardages listed are for the entire quilt as shown in the color photo on page 65. Instructions for each row indicate the yardage required for that row only.

1 fat quarter Fabric A (red poinsettia print) for Row 1

1 fat quarter Fabric B (green/red snowflake print) for Row 1

½ yd. Fabric C (cream snowflake print) for Rows 1 and 5

3¼ yds. Fabric D (green print) for filler strips, sashing, and Row 2

1⅜ yds. Fabric E (red snowflake print) for binding and Rows 2 and 5

⅛ yd. Fabric F (gold/red/green print) for Row 2

⅓ yd. Fabric G (red and green stripe) for Row 3

⅜ yd. Fabric H (cream/gold print) for Rows 3 and 6

⅓ yd. Fabric I (pine tree print) for Row 4

⅓ yd. Fabric J (tan/gold print) for Row 4

½ yd. Fabric K (small-scale green/red print) for Rows 5 and 6

¼ yd. Fabric L (rose plaid) for Row 6

⅛ yd. *each* of Fabrics M and N (pine cone prints) for Row 7

5¾ yds. fabric for backing

66" x 100" piece of batting

Cutting Sashing, Filler Strips, and Binding

NOTE: Cut all Fabric D sashing strips on the *lengthwise* grain (parallel to the selvage). Filler strips may be cut across the grain to make best use of the fabric. Set aside the remaining fabric for the pieced blocks.

All measurements include ¼"-wide seam allowances.

From Fabric D, cut:

8 strips, each 4½" x 62½", for sashing

NOTE: Label the following filler strips by row number.

4 strips, each 9½" x 27", for Rows 1 and 7

2 strips, each 9½" x 22½", for Row 2

2 strips, each 9½" x 18", for Row 3

2 strips, each 9½" x 13½", for Row 4

2 strips, each 9½" x 9", for Row 5

2 strips, each 9½" x 4½", for Row 6

From Fabric E, cut:

8 strips, each 4½" x 42", for binding

Cutting and Piecing the Rows

Refer to "Quiltmaking Basics" on page 6 for general construction techniques, and to the assembly diagram on page 72 for guidance as you piece each row.

All measurements include ¼"-wide seam allowances.

Row 1

Block Name: Right Hand of
    Friendship
Finished Block Size: 9"
1 fat quarter *each* of Fabrics A, B, and C

CUTTING

From *each* of Fabrics A and B, cut:
    1 square, 4¼" x 4¼"; cut square twice diagonally to make 4 triangles
    1 square, 3⅞" x 3⅞"; cut square once diagonally to make 2 triangles
From Fabric C, cut:
    1 square, 4¼" x 4¼"; cut square twice diagonally to make 4 triangles
    4 squares, each 3½" x 3½"

ASSEMBLY

1. Sew a large Fabric A and Fabric B triangle together on one short side as shown. Press seams toward Fabric A. Make 2.
2. Sew the 2 units from step 1 together as shown. Press seams to one side.
3. Sew a small Fabric B triangle to two neighboring sides of a 3½" Fabric C square. Press seams toward the triangles. Make 2.
4. Sew the unit from step 2 between the 2 units from step 3 as shown. Press seams away from the center square.
5. Sew a small Fabric A and Fabric C triangle together on one short side. Press seams toward Fabric A. Make 2 of each as shown in block diagram below.
6. Sew a unit from step 5 to 2 neighboring sides of a remaining 3½" Fabric C square as shown. Press seams toward the triangles. Make 2.
7. Sew the unit from step 4 between the 2 units from step 6. Press seams as desired.

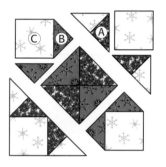
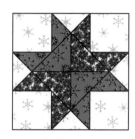

Make 1.

8. Position the finished block between two 9½" x 27" Fabric D filler strips, aligning the block sides with a short end of each strip. Sew the strips to the block, and press seams toward the strips.

Row 2

Block Name: Contrary Wife
Finished Block Size: 9"
⅛ yd. *each* of Fabrics D, E, and F

CUTTING

From *each* of Fabrics D and E, cut:
    4 squares, each 3⅞" x 3⅞"; cut squares once diagonally to make 8 triangles
From Fabric F, cut:
    10 squares, each 3½" x 3½"

ASSEMBLY

1. Sew a Fabric D and Fabric E triangle together along the long diagonal edge. Press seams toward the darker triangle. Make 8.

2. Sew a 3½" Fabric F square between 2 units from step 1 as shown. Press seams away from the center square. Make 2.

3. Sew a unit from step 1 between two 3½" Fabric F squares as shown. Press seams away from the Fabric F squares. Make 4.

4. Sew a unit from step 2 between 2 units from step 3 as shown. Press seams in opposite directions from block to block. Make 2.

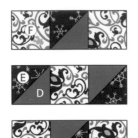 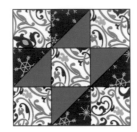

Make 2.

5. Join the 2 blocks as shown in the assembly diagram, rotating them so they resemble the top of a Christmas tree. Position the blocks between two 9½" x 22½" Fabric D filler strips, aligning the block sides with a short end of each strip. Sew the blocks and strips together, and press seams toward the strips.

Row 3

Block Name: Zigzag
Finished Block Size: 9"
⅓ yd. Fabric G; ¼ yd. Fabric H

CUTTING

From Fabric G, cut:

12 rectangles, each 2¾" x 5"

6 squares, each 3⅛" x 3⅛"; cut squares once diagonally to make 12 triangles

From Fabric H, cut:

12 squares, each 2¾" x 2¾"

6 squares, each 3⅛" x 3⅛"; cut squares once diagonally to make 12 triangles

ASSEMBLY

1. Sew a Fabric G and Fabric H triangle together along the long diagonal edge. Press seam toward Fabric G. Make 12.

2. Sew a 2¾" Fabric H square to each unit from step 1, taking care to position the triangles as shown. Press seams toward the step 1 units.

3. Sew a 2¾" x 5" Fabric G rectangle to each unit from step 2 as shown. Press seams toward the Fabric G rectangles.

4. Sew units from step 3 in pairs, taking care to position the units as shown. Press seams toward the Fabric G rectangles.

5. Sew units from step 4 in pairs as shown. Press seams in opposite directions from block to block. Make 3.

Make 3.

6. Join the 3 blocks in a horizontal row. Position them between the two 9½" x 18" Fabric D filler strips, aligning the block sides with a short end of each strip. Sew the blocks and strips together, and press seams toward the strips.

Row 4

Block Name: Sawtooth Star
Finished Block Size: 9"
⅓ yd. *each* of Fabrics I and J

CUTTING

From Fabric I, cut:

4 squares, each 5" x 5"

16 squares, each 3⅛" x 3⅛"; cut squares once diagonally to make 32 triangles

From Fabric J, cut:

4 squares, each 5¾" x 5¾"; cut squares twice diagonally to make 16 triangles

16 squares, each 2¾" x 2¾"

Assembly

1. With right sides together, sew a Fabric I triangle to the short left side of each Fabric J triangle as shown. Press seams toward Fabric I. Repeat to sew a Fabric I triangle to the short right side of the unit; press. Make 16.

2. Sew a 5" Fabric I square between 2 units from step 1 as shown. Press seams toward the center square. Make 4.

3. Sew a remaining unit from step 1 between two 2¾" Fabric J squares as shown. Press seams away from the Fabric J squares. Make 8.

4. Sew each unit from step 2 between 2 units from step 3. Press seams in opposite directions from block to block.

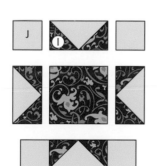

Make 4.

5. Join the 4 blocks in a horizontal row. Position them between the two 9½" x 13½" Fabric D filler strips, aligning the block sides with a short end of each strip. Sew the blocks and strips together, and press seams toward the strips.

Row 5

Block Name: Old Maid's Puzzle
Finished Block Size: 9"
⅜ yd. Fabric C; 1 fat quarter Fabric E; ⅛ yd. Fabric K

CUTTING

From Fabric C, cut:

5 squares, each 5⅜" x 5⅜"; cut squares once diagonally to make 10 triangles

10 squares, each 3⅛" x 3⅛"; cut squares once diagonally to make 20 triangles

20 squares, each 2¾" x 2¾"

From Fabric E, cut:

5 squares, each 5⅜" x 5⅜"; cut squares once diagonally to make 10 triangles

From Fabric K, cut:

10 squares, each 3⅛" x 3⅛"; cut squares once diagonally to make 20 triangles

ASSEMBLY

1. Sew a large Fabric C and Fabric E triangle together along the long diagonal edge. Press seams toward Fabric E. Make 10.

2. Sew a small Fabric C and Fabric K triangle together. Press seams toward Fabric K. Make 20.

3. Sew a unit from step 2 to each 2¾" Fabric C square, taking care to position the triangles as shown. Press the seams away from the Fabric C squares. Make 20.

4. Sew units from step 3 in pairs as shown. Press the seams to one side. Make 10.

5. Sew a unit from step 4 to each unit from step 1, taking care to position the triangles as shown. Press seams toward the step 1 units.

6. Sew units from step 5 in pairs as shown. Press seams to one side. Make 5.

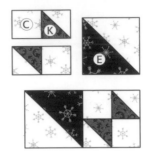

Make 5.

7. Join the 5 blocks in a horizontal row, rotating them as shown in the assembly diagram. Position the blocks between the two 9½" x 9" Fabric D filler strips, aligning the block sides with a 9½" end of each strip. Sew the blocks and strips together, and press seams toward the strips.

Row 6

Block Name: Thrifty
Finished Block Size: 9"
¼ yd. *each* of Fabrics H and L; ⅓ yd. Fabric K

CUTTING
From Fabric H, cut:
   3 strips, each 2" x 42"
From Fabric K, cut:
   6 squares, each 3½" x 3½"
   3 strips, each 2" x 42"
From Fabric L, cut:
   24 squares, each 3½" x 3½"

ASSEMBLY

1. With right sides together and long raw edges aligned, sew a 2" x 42" Fabric H strip and a 2" x 42" Fabric K strip together to make a 3½" x 42" strip set. Press seams toward Fabric K. Make 3 strip sets.

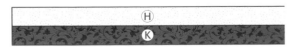

Make 3 strip sets.

2. Crosscut the strip sets into a total of 48 segments, each 2" wide.

Cut 48.

3. Sew units from step 2 in pairs as shown below. Press the seams to one side. Make 24.

4. Sew a 3½" Fabric L square between 2 units from step 3, taking care to position the units as shown. Press seams toward the Fabric L square. Make 12.

5. Sew each 3½" Fabric K square between 2 remaining 3½" Fabric L squares. Press seams toward Fabric L. Make 6.

6. Sew each unit from step 5 between 2 units from step 4. Press seams in 1 direction.

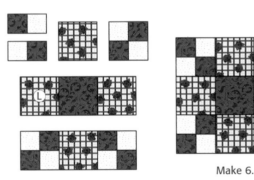
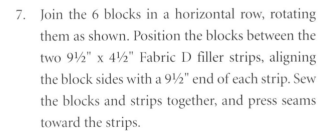

Make 6.

7. Join the 6 blocks in a horizontal row, rotating them as shown. Position the blocks between the two 9½" x 4½" Fabric D filler strips, aligning the block sides with a 9½" end of each strip. Sew the blocks and strips together, and press seams toward the strips.

Row 7

Block Name: Strip Block
Finished Block Size: 9"
⅛ yd. *each* of Fabrics M and N

CUTTING

From *each* of Fabrics M and N, cut:

3 strips, each 2" x 9½"

ASSEMBLY

1. Beginning with a Fabric M strip, lay out the 6 strips, alternating fabrics as shown. Sew the strips together along their long raw edges. Press seams to one side.

2. Position the finished block between the 2 remaining 9½" x 27" Fabric D filler strips, aligning the block sides with a short end of each strip. Sew the strips to the block, and press seams toward the strips.

QUILT ASSEMBLY

Refer to the assembly diagram on page 72. Arrange Rows 1–7 and the eight 4½" x 62½" Fabric D sashing strips as shown. With right sides together, and carefully matching centers and ends, pin and sew the rows and sashing together. Press seams toward the sashing strips.

> **Tip** A word of caution: Do not simply sew each row to the next without finding and matching the center points. Otherwise, your rows may "wander" and the tree shape won't be symmetrical. If the ends of the rows are uneven, they may straightened before the quilt is layered for basting.

FINISHING

Refer to "Quilting" and "Finishing" on pages 13–16.

1. Divide the backing fabric crosswise into 2 equal panels of approximately 104" each. Remove the selvages and join the pieces to make a single, large backing panel.

2. Center and layer the quilt top and the batting over the backing; baste.

3. Quilt as desired.

4. Trim the batting and backing even with the edges of the quilt top.

5. This quilt has a 1"-wide finished French double-fold binding. Use the 4½" x 42" Fabric E strips to make the binding. Lightly press the long raw edge of the binding over ¼". This crease becomes your ¼" seam guide for sewing the binding to the quilt.

6. Align the binding so that the ¼" seam guide is 1" from the raw edge of the quilt sandwich, and stitch on the crease. (You will actually be sewing 1" from the edge of the quilt). Remember to stop and turn 1" from each corner to ensure that the binding is even in width and filled with batting. Finish the binding as instructed in "Binding" on page 15.

7. Make and attach a label to your quilt.

Terry Martin, 1999, Snohomish, Washington, 45½" x 63"; machine quilted by Roxanne Carter.

74

▶ As a young girl, I spent summers with my grandparents in Walla Walla, Washington. They had a half-acre garden where my grandmother spent hours every day. The grounds near the house were filled with prize-winning flowers; the "back forty" included fruit trees and row upon row of different fruits and vegetables. All summer long, my grandmother would can the garden's bounty.

Instantly upon seeing the top for this quilt, my best friend, Cornelia, came up with the perfect name. We share a lot of childhood memories, and I was really touched that she remembered how fondly I think back on my summer days with Grandma and Grandpa.

The fabric choices in this quilt worried me. They all had a very strong presence, but I was determined that they work together. I wanted each row's colors to blend with the next, so I used pieced sashing rows instead of solid fabric to make the transition from one color group to the next. It was definitely a leap of faith to slap the top three rows together without sashing! However, I thought each strong block design, fabric choice, and color combination let the individual rows hold their own, even with such strong "neighbors."

Materials (42"-wide fabric)

NOTE: Yardages listed are for the entire quilt as shown in the color photo on page 73. Instructions for each row indicate the yardage for that row only.

½ yd. Fabric A (dark cherry print) for Rows 1 and 7

½ yd. Fabric B (tan cherry print) for Rows 1 and 6

1 fat quarter Fabric C (small red cherry print) for Rows 1 and 7

⅞ yd. Fabric D (red print) for sashing, binding, and Rows 2 and 6

⅓ yd. Fabric E (light tan print) for Row 2

⅓ yd. Fabric F (blue plaid) for Rows 2, 5, and 9

1 fat quarter Fabric G (feed sack print) for Row 2

⅜ yd. Fabric H (yellow check) for Rows 3 and 9

⅜ yd. Fabric I (vegetable print) for Row 3

⅔ yd. Fabric J (jar print) for Rows 4 and 8*

⅛ yd. Fabric K (blue print) for Rows 5 and 6

1 fat quarter Fabric L (white print) for Row 6

⅓ yd. Fabric M (cherry stripe) for Rows 6 and 8

2⅞ yds. fabric for backing

49" x 67" piece of batting

*This is a ballpark figure, based on the specific fabric I used. You may need to adjust this yardage (and/or piece the strip), depending upon whether the motif in your fabric runs across the width of the fabric or parallel to the selvage.

Cutting Sashing and Binding

All cutting measurements include ¼"-wide seam allowances.

From Fabric D, cut:

1 strip, 2½" x 45½", for sashing*

6 strips, each 2½" x 42", for binding

*You will need to piece this strip.

Cutting and Piecing the Rows

Refer to "Quiltmaking Basics" on page 6 for general construction techniques, and to the assembly diagram on page 78 for guidance as you piece each row.

All cutting measurements include ¼"-wide seam allowances.

Row 1

Block Name: Texas Puzzle

Finished Block Size: 9"

⅓ yd. *each* of Fabrics A and B; 1 fat quarter of Fabric C

CUTTING

From *each* of Fabrics A and B, cut:

10 squares, each 4⅞" x 4⅞; cut squares once diagonally to make 20 triangles

From Fabric C, cut:

10 strips, each 1½" x 4½"

5 strips, each 1½" x 9½"

ASSEMBLY

1. Sew a Fabric A and Fabric B triangle together along the long diagonal edge. Press seams toward Fabric A.

2. Sew a 1½" x 4½" Fabric C strip between 2 units from step 1. Make 6 units with the Fabric B triangle on the outside edges and 4 units with the Fabric A triangles on the outside edges. Press seams toward the Fabric C strips.

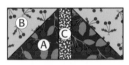

Make 6.   Make 4.

3. Sew a 1½" x 9½" Fabric C strip between 2 matching units from step 2 as shown. Press seams toward the Fabric C strip. Make 5.

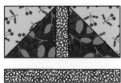

Make 5 blocks *total*.

4. Join the 5 blocks in a horizontal row, alternating the colors as shown. Sew the blocks together, and press seams to one side.

Row 2

Block Name: Cypress

Finished Block Size: 9"

1 fat quarter *each* of Fabrics D and G; ⅓ yd. Fabric E; ⅛ yd. Fabric F

CUTTING

From Fabric D, cut:

5 squares, each 5¾" x 5¾"; cut squares twice diagonally to make 20 triangles

From Fabric E, cut:

30 squares, each 3⅛" x 3⅛"; cut squares once diagonally to make 60 triangles

From Fabric F, cut:

10 squares, each 3⅛" x 3⅛"; cut squares once diagonally to make 20 triangles

From Fabric G, cut:

5 squares, each 5" x 5"

ASSEMBLY

1. Sew a Fabric E and Fabric F triangle together along the long diagonal edge. Press seams toward Fabric E. Make 20.

2. Sew a remaining Fabric E triangle to the short left side of each Fabric D triangle as shown. Press seams toward Fabric E. Repeat to sew a Fabric E triangle to the short right side of each unit; press.

3. Sew a unit from step 2 between 2 units from step 1, taking care to position the triangles as shown. Press seams toward the center of the unit. Make 10.

4. Sew each 5" Fabric G square between 2 remaining units from step 2 as shown. Press seams away from the Fabric G square. Make 5.

5. Sew each unit from step 4 between 2 units from step 3 as shown. Press seams in opposite directions from block to block.

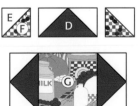

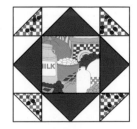

Make 5.

6. Join the 5 blocks in a horizontal row. Sew the blocks together, and press seams to one side.

76

Row 3

Block Name: Churn Dash
Finished Block Size: 9"
1 fat quarter Fabric H; ⅜ yd. Fabric I

CUTTING

From Fabric H, cut:

10 squares, each 3⅞" x 3⅞"; cut squares once diagonally to make 20 triangles

20 rectangles, each 2" x 3½"

From Fabric I, cut:

10 squares, each 3⅞" x 3⅞"; cut squares once diagonally to make 20 triangles

20 rectangles, each 2" x 3½"

5 squares, each 3½" x 3½"

ASSEMBLY

1. Sew a Fabric H and Fabric I triangle together along the long diagonal edge. Press seam toward Fabric I. Make 20.

2. Sew a 2" x 3½" Fabric H and Fabric I rectangle together along one long side. Press seams toward Fabric I. Make 20.

3. Sew a unit from step 2 between 2 units from step 1, taking care to position the triangles as shown. Press seams toward the center unit. Make 10.

4. Sew each 3½" Fabric I square between 2 remaining units from step 2 as shown. Press seams away from the Fabric I square.

5. Sew each unit from step 4 between 2 units from step 3 as shown. Press seams in opposite directions from block to block.

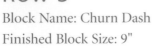
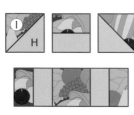

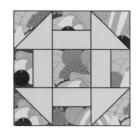

Make 5.

6. Join the 5 blocks in a horizontal row. Sew the blocks together, and press seams to one side.

Row 4

From Fabric J, cut:

1 panel or strip, 7½" x 45½"

NOTE: You may need to piece this horizontal strip. The fabric in the sample was fussy-cut so that the motif repeated "regularly" for the length of the strip.

Row 5

Finished Row Size: 45" x 3"
⅛ yd. *each* of Fabrics F and K

CUTTING

From Fabric F, cut:

10 squares, each 3½" x 3½"

From Fabric K, cut:

10 rectangles, each 2" x 3½"

ASSEMBLY

Beginning with a 2" x 3½" Fabric K rectangle, lay out the rectangles and 3½" Fabric F squares in a horizontal row, alternating them as shown in the assembly diagram. Sew the squares and rectangles together, and press seams to one side.

Row 6

Block Name: Children's Delight
Finished Block Size: 10"
Scrap of Fabric K; ⅛ yd. *each* of Fabrics D and B; 1 fat quarter *each* of Fabrics L and M

CUTTING

From Fabric K, cut:

4 squares, each 4½" x 4½"

4 squares, each 2½" x 2½"

From Fabric L, cut:

16 rectangles, each 2½" x 4½"

From Fabric D, cut:

16 squares, each 2½" x 2½"

From Fabric M, cut:

 8 strips, each 2½" x 8½"

From Fabric B, cut:

 5 strips, each 1½" x 10½"

ASSEMBLY

1. Sew each 4½" Fabric K square between two 2½" x 4½" Fabric L rectangles. Press seams toward Fabric K. Make 4.

2. Sew each remaining 2½" x 4½" Fabric L rectangle between two 2½" Fabric D squares. Press seams toward Fabric D. Make 8.

3. Sew each unit from step 1 between 2 units from step 2. Press the seams toward the center of the block.

4. Sew a 2½" x 8½" Fabric M strip to the left side of each unit from step 3. Press seams toward Fabric M.

5. Sew a 2½" Fabric K square to 1 short end of each remaining 2½" x 8½" Fabric M strip. Press seams toward the strip.

6. Sew a unit from step 5 to the bottom edge of each unit from step 4 as shown. Press seams toward the bottom unit.

7. Sew a 1½" x 10½" Fabric B strip to the left edge of each block as shown. Press seams toward the Fabric B strips.

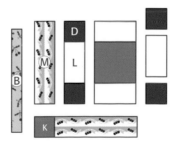 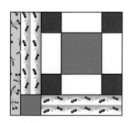

Make 4.

8. Join the 4 blocks in a horizontal row. Finish the row with the remaining 1½" x 10½" Fabric B strip as shown. Sew the blocks and strip together and press seams to one side.

Row 7

Row Name: Sawtooth
Finished Row Size: 45" x 3"
⅛ yd. *each* of Fabrics A and C

CUTTING

From *each* of Fabrics A and C, cut:

 9 squares, each 3⅜" x 3⅜"; cut squares once diagonally to make 18 triangles

ASSEMBLY

1. Sew a Fabric A and Fabric C triangle together along the long diagonal edge. Press seam toward Fabric A. Make 18.

2. Join the 18 units in a horizontal row, taking care to position the triangles as shown in the assembly diagram. Sew the units together, and press seams in one direction.

Row 8

Finished Row Size: 45" x 8"
Fabric J (see note in "Cutting" below); ¼ yd. Fabric M

CUTTING

From Fabric J, cut:

 1 panel or strip, 6½" x 45½" (You may need to piece this horizontal strip. The fabric in the sample was fussy-cut so that the motif repeated "regularly" for the length of the strip.)

From Fabric M, cut:

 3 strips, each 1½" x 42"

ASSEMBLY

1. Sew the 1½" x 42" Fabric M strips together, end to end, to make a continuous 1½"-wide strip. From this strip, cut two 1½" x 45½" strips.

2. With right sides together, and matching centers and ends, pin and sew the 6½" x 45½" Fabric J panel between the two 1½" x 45½" Fabric M strips. Press seams toward the Fabric J panel.

78

Row 9

Row Name: Checkerboard
Finished Row Size: 45" x 3"
¼ yd. *each* of Fabrics F and H

CUTTING

From *each* of Fabrics F and H, cut:
 2 strips, each 2" x 42"

ASSEMBLY

1. With right sides together and long raw edges aligned, sew a 2" x 42" Fabric F and Fabric H strip together to make a 3½" x 42" strip set. Press seams toward Fabric F. Make 2 strip sets.

Make 2 strip sets.

2. Crosscut the strip sets into a total of 30 segments, each 2" wide.

Cut 30.

3. Join the 30 segments from step 2, taking care to position them as shown. Sew the segments together, and press seams to one side.

QUILT ASSEMBLY

Refer to the assembly diagram (right). Arrange Rows 1–9 as shown. Place the 2½" x 45½" Fabric D sashing strip between Rows 3 and 4. With right sides together, and matching centers and ends, pin and sew the rows together. Press seams in one direction.

FINISHING

Refer to "Quilting" and "Finishing" on pages 13–16.

1. Divide the backing fabric crosswise into 2 equal panels of approximately 52" each. Remove the selvages and join the pieces to make a single, large backing panel.

2. Position the backing so the seam runs horizontally. Center and layer the quilt top and the batting over the backing; baste.

3. Quilt as desired.

4. Trim the batting and backing even with the edges of the quilt top. Use the 2½" x 42" Fabric D strips to make the binding; sew the binding to the quilt.

5. Make and attach a label to your quilt.

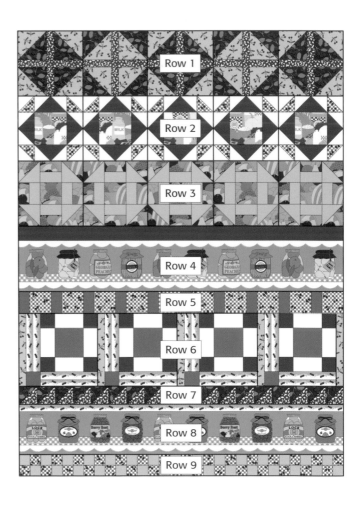

Block Index

Alphabet/Number Chart

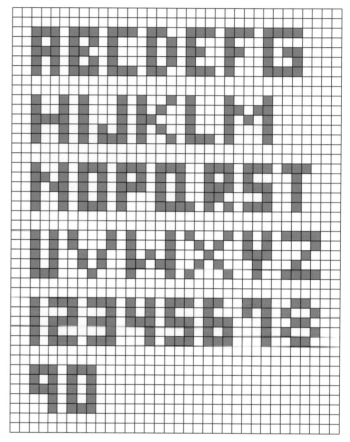

Bibliography

Hopkins, Judy. *Around the Block with Judy Hopkins: 200 Rotary-Cut Blocks in 6 Sizes.* Bothell, Wash.: Martingale & Company, 1994.

Brackman, Barbara. *Encyclopedia of Pieced Quilt Patterns.* Paducah, Ky.: American Quilter's Society, 1993.

Martin, Nancy J. *365 Quilt Blocks a Year.* Bothell, Wash.: Martingale & Company, 1999.

Reikes, Ursula. *More Quilts for Baby.* Bothell, Wash.: Martingale & Company, 1997.

About the Author

Since the time she was shown how a needle pierces cloth and told that fabric was called "material," Terry Martin has had a love affair with sewing. Except for the basics her grandmother Gammy taught her, she is a self-taught manipulator of thread and cloth. In those days "back when," nothing gave her more joy than discovering that chubby girls could sew their own fashion clothes. From garment sewing, cross-stitch, embroidery, and needlepoint, she has continued her infatuation with the fabric arts through quilting. Her love of fabric (of which no one, she says, can have too much!) is right behind her love for family, friends, and choco-late—and for Terry, that's saying something.